Learning
to Teach
Mathematics

Maria Goulding

David Fulton Publishers
London

David Fulton Publishers Ltd
Ormond House, 26–27 Boswell Street, London WC1N 3JD

First published in Great Britain by David Fulton Publishers 1997

British Library Cataloguing in Publication Data
A catalogue record for this book is available from the British Library

ISBN 1–85346–459–7

Typeset by Sheila Knight, London
Printed in Great Britain by the Cromwell Press Limited, Melksham

Contents

To Pete, for keeping me writing,
and Peter, Anna and Alison for encouraging me

Introduction

The teaching and learning of mathematics is dogged with controversy. On the one hand, the importance of the subject as a core subject in the curriculum is legitimised in school curricula across the world. On the other, opinions about how it should be taught, whether standards are rising or falling, and what we should include in the written curriculum are fiercely debated. In the Western world, such arguments are played out against a backdrop of substantial lack of confidence amongst the adult population, to the point at which people claim to experience panic and fear when asked to perform 'school-like' mathematical calculations.

A colleague and I recently attempted to find out what prospective primary teachers could remember from their days of school mathematics to inform the planning of subject knowledge sessions during the course. Some were outraged and suggested that we should have given them a chance to revise! This contrasts with the teaching of English which also attracts concern about performance in terms of reading and spelling, but which does not seem to induce the same feelings of bewilderment and unease as mathematics. That mathematics should be seen on the one hand as extremely important and useful but on the other as abstract, difficult and obscure is a great dilemma for all those engaged in its teaching.

But not all is doom and gloom. Many people do not realise that although entries for 'A' level Mathematics in England and Wales have declined in the last ten years, they are second only to English and that the modal grade obtained is high – A in 1994. So there are successful mathematicians, and those who enter teaching often want to share their own enthusiasm and confidence in the subject. They will of course be preoccupied with many of the concerns felt by students of other subjects, but there will be concerns particularly pertinent to them as mathematics teachers. These are the focus for this book.

Given that the mathematics curriculum in England and Wales is now prescribed and statutory, students on training courses will have to know the National Curriculum Orders for Mathematics. These orders do not prescribe how to teach, so in addition, there are several very good books (e.g. Backhouse *et al.*, 1992) which student teachers of mathematics should also consult. These will give a much fuller picture of the complexity of teaching and learning mathematics and will help students move beyond simplistic notions. It is a salutary fact that there is still a great deal we do not know about the teaching and learning of mathematics, but the recent report commissioned by the Office for Standards in Education (Askew and Wiliam, 1995) goes some way towards presenting research findings in a form accessible to student teachers. I would expect students to use this booklet regularly and have made references to it at several points in this book.

In this book, however, I wish to complement the work of others by focusing on student teachers – how they make sense of their experiences, how they learn about teaching and learning, and how they cope with the stresses and strains of their training. This will be done largely by using a variety of information sources collected from Post-Graduate Certificate of Education (PGCE) secondary mathematics students over the period of a year. By using this material readers may see echoes of their own experience, identify possibilities which they may like to try, and find support in the accounts of recently qualified PGCE students. Running alongside this are references to the research on how students learn to be teachers of mathematics. It seems to me that this research is written up largely for an audience of teacher educators, when in fact student teachers have a great deal to learn from it as well. There is a great deal we still do not know about this process and those of us who are teacher educators need to share our uncertainties with students.

Not all the personal accounts paint a positive picture. The recently established school-based courses of teacher education are far from perfect, and the problems of obtaining consistency of experience while preserving diversity are unlikely ever to be solved. With so many schools and so much relying on good communications, there will always be disagreements about judgements and personality clashes as well as temporary difficulties owing to sickness or domestic upheaval. In principle, though, the benefits of school and the Institute of Higher Education (IHE) working together to prepare new teachers in a complementary and developmental way should outweigh the disadvantages. At a practical level, the fact that schools are now paid for their part of the training and that quality assurance schemes are in place is a welcome step forward.

Prospective teachers should know, however, that the new arrangements can be viewed as a political device to weaken the professional status of teaching, to dilute the influence of higher education with its emphasis on research and to reduce the practice of teaching to a set of observable skills. This view is strengthened by the knowledge that the moves to school-based training have been inadequately funded and supported. So the reader will find evidence of tension and disappointment in some of the accounts, together with positive pictures of genuine support and progress.

The main audience for this book will be intending teachers of secondary mathematics, although student teachers of older pupils in primary school and student teachers of mathematics in middle schools will also find much which is useful. With this in mind, the book is structured in three parts, to reflect the developing interests and concerns of such students as they progress throughout their training year. In part one, the chapters deal with the first steps of socialisation into the training institution and the first teaching schools, an overview of the way in which development may take place over the year, and an introduction to the statutory curriculum and its assessment, which provides the framework within which school mathematics departments operate.

In the second part, data from lesson observations, interviews and other sources will bring alive the critical experiences of the year: learning how to manage pupils, to plan, execute and evaluate lessons and to use professional feedback and advice constructively. Accounts of real lessons, examples of real lesson plans, and extracts from real feedback interviews will be used here.

In my experience, some of the important insights gained from research into children's mathematical thinking and from the writing concerned with the social and political context of mathematics teaching is lost on students at the beginning of their course, when survival is the highest priority. If some attempt is not made to return to these dimensions, there is a danger that the student will never give them due attention. I have therefore pursued these issues in part three, although many will have surfaced in previous chapters. Some readers may wish to start with this section or to dip into it as they progress through the earlier parts.

I have thought long and hard about the best place for what is now the first chapter. It contains some important background to the present curriculum for schools in England and Wales, together with straightforward factual information. My impressions are that many students who apply for teacher education courses are hampered by their ignorance of the framework within which mathematics is taught in schools, and unaware of the controversies which surround it. So the leading position given to the chapter does not imply that the curriculum and its assessment is more important than other issues, but that they are both very influential in shaping the mathematical experiences of pupils in schools. I hope this chapter will enable students to see opportunities as well as constraints within the present system.

Students at the beginning of the course may expect the IHE to be the place where they learn about the theory of education, and schools where they will learn about the practice. There is an element of truth in this division. I hope, however, to present a more integrated picture and to provide the reader with a supportive and informative account which helps them to make sense of teaching and learning, to clarify their thinking, to consider possible alternatives, and to begin to make informed and intelligent choices in their classrooms, staffrooms and schools.

In writing this book, I am drawing from over 10 years' experience of teacher education. Observed lessons, conversations, lectures, seminars, research done and read have all fed into it, but the research conducted over 1994–95 is the backbone of the work. I need to thank the many students from that cohort whose lessons I observed, whose lessons plans and profiles I borrowed, and in particular those who gave up their time to be interviewed. In the interests of confidentiality, I have used pseudonyms for students and teachers, but unfortunately I cannot hide behind a pseudonym myself. Many of the transcriptions and examples of data have revealed to me aspects of my own practice which would have remained unexamined otherwise. Reading these closely has been a revelatory and often uncomfortable experience for me, but one from which I continue to learn. This is the spirit in which the book is offered. It is not meant to be a model of ideal practice, rather an invitation to explore the induction of new mathematics teachers from a critical and constructive perspective.

REFERENCES

Askew, M. and Wiliam, D. (1995) *Ofsted Review of Recent Research in Mathematics Education 5–16.* London: HMSO.

Backhouse, J., Haggerty, L., Pirie, S. and Stratton, J. (1992) *Improving the Learning of Mathematics.* London: Cassell.

Department for Education (1995) *Mathematics in the National Curriculum.* London: HMSO.

Part 1: Beginnings

1: The mathematics curriculum in schools

BACKGROUND

Before the National Curriculum was devised in the late 1980s, the curriculum in primary schools and the lower years of secondary schools was the responsibility of schools and individual teachers with guidance from the local authority. In practice, the widespread use of popular textbook schemes and the standardised tests which were used by local authorities to monitor performance meant that there was a degree of conformity. Of course in the later secondary years, examination syllabuses – the General Certificate of Education 'O' and 'A' levels, the Certificate of Secondary Education, and in 1988 the General Certificate of Secondary Education – had a strongly defining influence on the content and practice of mathematics teaching.

In mathematics, the intellectual ferment of the 1960s and 1970s had given rise to several curriculum development projects, e.g. Nuffield in the primary schools, and the School Mathematics Project in the secondary school, and these had an impact on educational thought and practice in some schools. An early attempt at drawing up a basic list of content in mathematics can be found in the foundation list for low attainers in *Mathematics Counts*, the famous Cockcroft report of the early 1980s. But the main aim of that work was:

> To consider the teaching of mathematics in primary and secondary schools in England and Wales, with particular regard to the mathematics required in further and higher education, employment and adult life generally . . . .

Although a mathematics report, many of the ideas in Cockcroft were used in setting up the GCSE, a system designed to get rid of the unfortunate division between 'O' levels and CSE grades by unifying the examinations for 16 year olds. With the GCSE also came the opportunity for coursework, which gave teachers responsibility for part of the assessed work of the examination. This in turn was a development of the Mode Three CSE syllabuses in which some schools had written their own syllabuses and continuously assessed their pupils' work, under the authority of an examination board.

THE NATIONAL CURRICULUM

Hard on the heels of the GCSE and not long after the prolonged conflict over teachers' pay in the 1980s, the Education Reform Act of 1988 ushered in the National Curriculum. The aim of the legislation was to provide a curriculum framework, national assessment for pupils aged from 5 to 16, to be used both for assessing pupils and the performance of schools. Students starting their training now will have lived through the enormous changes and arguments surrounding these changes but none of this will be apparent when they open the present set of orders (DfE, 1995). They may well wonder what all the fuss has been about, and secretly relieved that the 60 pages devoted to the first Mathematics version has now been reduced to a manageable 30.

A short review of the story here is interesting and appropriate, since it will give students some understanding of the pressures which have shaped the official curriculum which will shape their teaching.

The introduction of a legally binding curriculum and its associated assessment was felt necessary in order to improve standards in schools and to provide pupils with an entitlement curriculum. This was one strand of the 1988 Act, which also paved the way for delegated school budgets, new kinds of school , the reintroduction of selection, teacher appraisal and OFSTED (Office for Standards in Education) inspections, amongst other things. Clearly all these changes are controversial and were politically motivated to reduce the power of the local education authorities, to make teachers more accountable and to publicise inspection judgements about schools.

In comparison with those issues, a clearly defined curriculum for mathematics may seem relatively innocuous, with perhaps some worries about the way in which it is assessed and the use to which the assessment results can be put. But leaving aside the assessment question, even the construction of the mathematics curriculum has been contentious and subject to interference. Is this just arguing for the sake of it or are there important issues at stake?

One argument which caught the popular imagination centred around long multiplication and long division. The working party who drew up the initial report were a distinguished group of 20 members from local authorities, universities, primary, secondary and tertiary colleges, and representatives of research bodies, industry and a training service. After careful consideration of the variety of calculation methods they wanted to see – a balance between mental, written and calculator methods – one of their conclusions was that: 'We believe that it is unnecessary to teach pencil and paper techniques for long division and multiplication'. This was one recommendation which was too much for the then Secretary of State for Education. Non-calculator methods for multiplying and dividing three-digit numbers by two-digit numbers were inserted into the 1989 orders and have remained ever since.

It is important to tell this small story, even though it clearly concerns only a fragment of the number curriculum. Some things, like the long division algorithm, or the ability to spell chrysanthemum, or to know the date of the Battle of Agincourt, can assume an almost symbolic importance around which a set of beliefs, attitudes and opinions can cluster. If adults have struggled to learn something then they may attach too much importance to those items. They begin to stand for far more than they are worth, and people can be polarised into two camps in a destructive and time-consuming battle for ascendancy. The working party had come to their conclusion knowing that:

- Many pupils fail to use long multiplication and long division methods accurately even after extensive drilling.
- *Being able to do* the method does not mean that a pupil would necessarily know *when to do* that method.
- Most people in adult life would automatically reach for a calculator to multiply three-digit numbers by two-digit numbers.
- If you spend less time in repetitive drill, it leaves time for higher order thinking and problems.

But these rational arguments failed to win the day, and nostalgia prevailed. No matter – pupils can still devise their own methods for these calculations and if teachers need to do some cramming before the tests then that is not very disastrous. It is the public perception which is potentially dangerous. There are still opportunities for the higher order mathematical activities which are possible with the aid of the calculator. The compulsory non-calculator test which will be introduced in 1997 may be seen at worst as a sop to politicians and at best it may lead to good practice in mental and written work.

Although the law does not stipulate how the curriculum should be organised or taught, the way in which the first mathematics orders were written did imply an assessment led delivery, or 'teaching to the test'. Other subjects made a clear distinction between:

- *Programmes of study* (what pupils should be taught)

and

- *Attainment targets* (what they should be tested on)

but in mathematics they were essentially the same thing. In the original orders there were 14 attainment targets, with discrete statements of attainment (illuminated by non-statutory examples), arranged into 10 levels. These were to be the basis of the assessment tests, so that there was a strong incentive to teach in a piecemeal way in order to target testable items. For instance, work on angles appeared in different parts of the curriculum.

Attainment Target 8: Measures,
Level 5 'measure and draw angles to the nearest degree'

Attainment Target 10: Shape and Space,
Level 4 'understand and use language associated with angles'
        Example: know acute, obtuse, and reflex angles . . .

Level 5 'explain and use angle properties associated with intersecting and parallel lines'
Example: identify equal angles in a diagram . . .

and nowhere in that version did we have reference to what an angle is, why angles are important and when they could be used, apart from one example of an investigation:

Attainment target 9: Using and Applying Mathematics,
Level 6 Example: Investigate the maximum number of right angles in polygons with different numbers of sides

Compare the treatment of angles in the second version (DES, 1991), when the 14 attainment targets had been reduced to five, and measurement had found a home with Shape and Space (Table 1.1).

Table 1.1 Level 2

Programme of study	Statements of attainment	Examples
Pupils should engage in activities which involve:	Pupils should be able to:	Pupils could:
• recognising squares, rectangles, circles, triangles, hexagons, pentagons, cubes, rectangular boxes(cuboids), cylinders and spheres and describing their properties	(a) Use mathematical terms to describe common 2D shapes and 3D objects	Create pictures and patterns using 2D shapes and describe them. Describe 3D objects using appropriate language.
• recognising right-angled corners in 2D and 3D shapes		
• recognising types of movement: straight (translation), turning (rotation)	(b) Recognise different types of movement	Rotate body through 1, 2, 3, and 4 right angles. Turn to left or right on instructions (in PE, games, using turtle graphics or programmable toys)
• understanding angles as a measurement of turn		
• understanding turning through right angles		

This does seem more coherent, at least as far as angles are concerned, and there is some attempt to distinguish between the Programmes of Study and the Statements of Attainment. It has to be remembered that teachers were working to the first set of curriculum orders before they knew what the tests would look like, and for many this was a disorienting experience. Some welcome advice became available with the publication of the National Curriculum Council's Non-Statutory guidance in 1989, and with the trickle of publications on assessment and record keeping from the School Examinations and Assessment Council.

THE NON-STATUTORY GUIDANCE

For many educators the non-statutory guidance was, and still remains, the nearest to a set of guiding principles and useful advice in interpreting and implementing the National Curriculum. For instance, it recommends that activities should:

- Bring together different areas of mathematics.
- Be ordered flexibly.
- Be balanced between tasks which develop knowledge, skills and understanding, and those which develop the ability to tackle practical problems.
- Be balanced between the applications of mathematics and ideas which are purely mathematical.
- Be balanced between those which are short in duration and those which have scope for development over an extended period.
- Where appropriate, use pupils' own interests or questions either as starting points or as further lines of development.
- Where appropriate, involve both independent and cooperative work.
- Be both of the kind which have an exact result or answer and those which have many possible outcomes.
- Be balanced between different modes of learning: doing, observing, talking and listening, discussing with other pupils, reflecting, drafting, reading and writing.
- Encourage pupils to use mental arithmetic and to become confident in the use of a range of mathematical tools.
- Enable pupils to communicate their mathematics.
- Enable pupils to develop their personal qualities.
- Enable pupils to develop a positive attitude to mathematics.

(NCC *Non-Statutory Guidance*, 1989, B8–B10)

Another important message was that pupils should develop a range of methods for calculating: mental, paper and pencil, and calculator methods. The idea was that they should adopt a balanced approach, being able to tackle calculations but also be able to:

- estimate
- approximate
- interpret answers
- check for reasonableness.

Many of these skills contribute to numeracy in its fullest sense, and it was recommended that 'the heavy emphasis placed on teaching standard written methods for calculations in the past needs to be re-examined'.

The non-statutory guidance also gave heart to people who felt that the new curriculum would result in dry teaching methods and closed tasks. For instance, it was very helpful to have examples of two teaching strategies which could both be used in planning:

1. Start with a task and then analyse it with respect to the PoS. For example, make a model with the largest possible surface area from six interlinking cubes joined

together. (Pupils aged 10–12, at the transition between KS3 and KS4.)

2. Start with an element of the PoS and then design activities relating to it. For example, 'Recognising squares, rectangles, circles etc.' With 6–7 year olds, the teacher could use Poleidoblocs, Logiblocs etc. and do this orally with questions like: 'Can you find a hexagon?', 'Please find me another of these' (indicating a shape).

Also memorable was the set of examples which illustrated how common closed tasks could be modified to produce more open and challenging tasks. For example:

Closed task   *Modified task*

Find the area of this triangle   Construct some triangles with
                                        the same area as this one.

Students would do well to read the non-statutory guidance alongside the current orders since it still has much to offer in terms of sound planning advice and the principles of good practice.

THE DEARING REVIEW

Looking back, the implementation of the National Curriculum and its assessment does seem lamentable. Uproar over the impracticability of the first testing for 7 year olds, never mind its desirability, and the boycott of tests for 14 year olds led to a serious rethink. Ron Dearing was the man brought in to oversee a wholesale review, this time taking great trouble to act on extensive public consultations. He found widespread support for the National Curriculum from a majority of teachers, but serious concern about curriculum overload. For mathematics, this review brought out a set of proposals which, after consultation, became the 1995 orders and a promise of no change for 5 years. The revised structure is summarised in Table 1.2.

Even a cursory look at the 1995 orders reveals a major shift in the mathematics curriculum, with a very clear separation of programmes of study from attainment targets, which appear at the back of the booklet. Although phrases common to both are detectable, the structure is very different, with no reference to progression through levels in the programmes of study. This at least provides a more rounded picture at the outset, although teachers who have been conditioned to think in terms of levels may find it hard to shake free of this mindset. The review was set up to simplify and slim down the curriculum – in fact it is slightly longer than the 1991 version, despite omissions and a severe reduction in the number of non-statutory examples which were so helpful in interpreting the statements of attainment. The student teacher

Table 1.2 Mathematics in the National Curriculum 1996: summary

Key stages	Age	Year	Programmes of study	Attainment targets	Method of assessment	Levels for vast majority
1	5–7	1, 2	Using and applying Mathematics	AT1 Using and applying mathematics	Teacher assessment (TA)	1–3
			Number	AT2 Number and algebra	National Assessment Tests/	
			Shape, space and measures	AT3 Shape, space and measures	Tasks and TA	
2	7–11	3, 4, 5, 6	Using and applying Mathematics	AT1	TA	2–5
			Number	AT2	Tests, TA	
			Shape, space and measures	AT3	Tests, TA	
			Handling data	AT4 Handling data	Tests, TA	
3	11–14	7, 8, 9	As KS 2	AT1	TA	3–8
				ATs, 2, 3, 4	Tests, TA	+ exceptional performance
4	14–16	10, 11	As KS 3 plus further material		GCSE	Not applicable GCSE grades are A*-G

would do well to look up all the examples from the 1991 orders, as they could still be used as good classroom starters:

> Investigate the possible total amount of money they may have when told someone has exactly three coins. (AT1 L3)

> Test the validity of statements such as 'Rectangles with the same area have the same perimeter' ... (AT1 L4)

> Use a calculator to find out which countries use most and least of the world's energy resources per capita. (AT2 L7)

Another major change was the use of *level descriptions* in the attainment targets. Instead of expecting pupils to be able to pass assessments of all, or all except one, of the criteria for a level, the idea is that the level description illustrates the performance of a typical pupil at that level, rather than specifying exactly what must be mastered.

USING AND APPLYING MATHEMATICS

There was one major source of contention during the consultation period of the Dearing review, which is still relevant. In the proposals, there were two versions:

- One with *Using and Applying Mathematics* as a separate section with its own attainment target and level statements.

- Another with *Using and Applying Mathematics* integrated into the programmes of study and, as an example, into the *Number and Algebra* targets.

There were good reasons why the second version should be done – separating out the 'content' part of the curriculum from the 'process' part could be seen as artificial. Pupils should be learning how to apply their knowledge, to communicate it and to develop powers of reasoning and proof in the context of number, algebra, shape and space, and handling data. Separating out this section could be seen as making process elements a bolt-on extra. The argument for integration did not succeed although it was close. Those who wanted to retain Using and Applying as a separate section had very real fears that if it was integrated it would be lost and we would return to a curriculum in which many of the innovative gains in investigative and problem solving work would be lost. Moreover, unless this kind of work was assessed in its own right it could be seen as marginal. So we have kept the Using and Applying element separate, with the proviso that it should permeate the other content elements, and that teachers should be responsible for its assessment.

ASSESSING MATHEMATICS IN THE NATIONAL CURRICULUM

As I write this section, the first national league tables of 11-year-old pupils' test results have been published. In these, local schools have been ranked according to the performance of pupils in the 1996 Mathematics, English and Science tests. In each column the percentage of pupils attaining level 4 or above in each of the core subjects is recorded, and the ranking is based on an aggregate score.

	English	Maths	Science	Rank
Tumbledown County Primary	35	37	44	104
Leafy Lane County Primary	98	93	86	3

Level 4 is described as the 'attainment . . . which the government deems an 11 year old should have reached to be performing satisfactorily' in a local paper, and in a national broadsheet both as 'the achievement expected of a typical 11 year old' and 'the level officially expected of all children of that age'. There is clearly some slippage of terminology here, with potentially serious consequences. It is a long way from the 1987 report from the Test Group on Assessment and Testing (TGAT) which offered 'best guesses' for the expected performance of pupils at each of the first three key stages:

KS1 2   (80% lying in the range 1–3)
KS2 4   (80% lying in the range 2–6)
KS3 5/6 (80% lying in the range 4–8)
KS4 7   (80% lying in the range 5–10)

Since these levels and the performance of the average child was being decided ahead of time they could never be more than predictions, but it is clear that the percentage of pupils attaining these 'average' levels is expected to rise in the drive for higher standards. Trying to track an upwards trend has been very difficult so far because there have been major changes both to the curriculum and to the assessments since they were first done in Key Stage 1 in 1991. Some of the most recent changes are included in the following section.

SUMMARY OF KEY STAGE 3 ASSESSMENT ARRANGEMENTS

At the time of writing, the latest changes to the national tests are the introduction of a non-calculator paper, and the piloting of a short mental arithmetic test. These have been deemed necessary by a general concern for numeracy and by the difficulty in previous years of specifying some questions where a calculator could be used and others where pupils had to use alternative methods. So now answers in index form, or the use of surds or multiples of pi will be accepted on this paper.

As before, pupils will be entered in different tiers: Levels 3–5, Levels 4–6, Levels 5–7, and Levels 6–8 (2 papers, 1 hour each). Compensatory levels can be awarded for those who *narrowly* fail to achieve the lowest level of the tier.

There will also be:

- An optional extension paper available for pupils entered for the highest tier.
- Optional tasks which can be done under classroom conditions for the small number of pupils at this key stage who are working at levels 1–2.

For certain pupils, e.g. those with a special needs statement, or those with English as an additional language, special arrangements may be given automatically or requested ahead of time, to give maximum access to the tests. These include the use of readers or amanuenses, the provision of extra time, the use of a separate room, or separating the tests into sections to allow for breaks (SCAA, 1996a).

Teacher assessment

Teachers are expected to give each pupil a level for each of the four attainment targets, and then find an average level, with the number and algebra attainment targets having a double weighting. How this is done is a professional matter for schools, as the only legal requirement is for yearly updated records, with academic achievements alongside other information, for each pupil. It is expected, however, that teachers should be able to judge these best fit levels over a range of contexts and activities and over time. The twist here is that the test results will be returned to schools before the Teacher Assessment levels are finalised, so it would be theoretically possible, but very poor practice, for a school to base its Teacher Assessment levels on the test results.

Reporting

Both the Teacher Assessment level and the Test level should be given alongside each other in reports to parents together with comparative school and national information. Both levels should also be sent for the national data collection.

HOW THE LEVELS ARE DETERMINED

Over time there has been a significant shift in the assessment of the national tests, from a criterion referenced system in which pupils had to fulfil specific criteria for the award of a level, to one in which the tests are mark- based. With the use of the broader level descriptions we now have a less mechanical illustration of performance, as opposed to a strict specification of what must be mastered. This means that decisions have to be made about converting the marks from tests into levels, and deciding what is the lowest acceptable mark needed to show competence in whatever is being assessed at that level. SCAA (the School Curriculum and Assessment Authority) use a system in which experienced teachers judge these cut-off scores, based on their knowledge of how minimally competent candidates (i.e. those judged to have just satisfied the level description) would be expected to perform on the tests.

FEEDBACK TO TEACHERS

SCAA provide yearly reports on the national tests, in which they provide general comments of interest to teachers.

Key Stage 2

In the report of the 1995 Key Stage 2 tests and tasks in the core subjects general features of the pupils' performance were summarised. For example:

- Questions requiring explanations or reasons were not always answered well.
- Children were not always familiar with the mathematical language necessary to understand and answer the questions (SCAA, 1996b: 17).

and there is an analysis of pupils' answers, illustrating typical errors and strategies. Drawn from these are the following implications for teaching and learning.

Number
For instance, when calculating the cost of 7 drinks at 48p and 8 drinks each at 52p both a short multiplication method and the more lengthy repeated addition methods were both evidenced:

$$
\begin{array}{ccc}
48 & 52 & 48 \\
\underline{\times\,7} & \underline{\times\,8} & 48 \\
336 & 416 & 48 \\
{\scriptstyle 5} & {\scriptstyle 1} & 48 \\
 & & 48 \\
 & & 48 \\
 & & \underline{48} \\
 & & 336 \\
 & & {\scriptstyle 5}
\end{array}
$$

and prompted the following advice:

> . . . [there is a] need for teaching to strike a balance between encouraging children to have the confidence to develop their own methods for doing calculations and providing them with straightforward and efficient standard methods which avoid time consuming and unnecessarily laborious work.

It is not clear of course if the pupils using long-winded methods on the tests had been taught standard methods but had not used them, but this comment is an interesting development from the advice given in the non-statutory guidance mentioned previously, with a move back to recommending the teaching of some 'efficient' standard methods.

Algebra

> . . . children need to be given more opportunities to explore sequences and relationships particularly when expressed as spatial patterns.

Space and shape

> Children need to have experience in making 3D models and know how simple 3D shapes can be constructed from a net.

Data handling and probability

> More emphasis needs to be placed on estimating proportions of data particularly when presented in the form of pie charts.

> [children need to] discuss different ways of explaining *why* a certain outcome has particular likelihoods associated with it.

This is all interesting advice for helping teachers to help pupils do better on the test, and some of the recommendations do chime in with the principles involved in the choice of activities recommended by the *Non-Statutory Guidance*.

Key Stage 3

The report on the 1996 Key Stage 3 assessments is a much briefer document and includes some information on the results of the tests, e.g. '56% of pupils achieving the standard expected of 14-year-old pupils (Level 5 or above)'. The decision to introduce the non-calculator test for the following year had already been made and the implications for teaching and learning reflect a shift back towards the teaching of the standard methods of calculation:

> Pupils need to be taught a range of strategies and algorithms for carrying out multiplication and division without a calculator . . .

Other teacher and learning implications range from the very wide to the very particular:

- Pupils need greater exposure to being required to communicate their understanding of mathematical concepts in words and diagrams and to use simple sentences.
- Pupils need opportunities to develop a more secure understanding of fractions and of algebra.
- Pupils need to be familiar with the metric equivalents of Imperial units still in daily life. These include: miles to kilometres (and vice versa) etc.
- Pupils need greater experience of handling data and interpreting tables of data, particularly with respect to cumulative frequency data.

GCSE MATHEMATICS

In England and Wales, most pupils in Key Stage 4 will be studying for their General Certificate of Secondary Education in several subjects. In mathematics, each of the five examination boards offers more than one syllabus which have to be approved by SCAA (School Curriculum and Assessment Authority). These have to accord with the National Curriculum Orders but achievement is reported by the grades G, F, E, D, C, B, A, up to A*. Again the weighting for assessment is:

Using and applying (Ma1)	20%
Number and algebra (Ma2)	40%
Shape, space and measures (Ma3)	20%
Handling data (Ma4)	20%

with the expectation that over time the questions will be monitored to make sure that they address the full range of content in these areas. Presently there are moves to stipulate a core of common questions across the examinations set by all the five boards.

Exceptionally, mathematics has three tiers of entry:

Foundation	awarding grades G–D
Intermediate	E–B
Higher	C–A*.

Unlike English which can offer up to 40% coursework, mathematics has the lowest ceiling of 20%. For non-modular schemes the terminal examination has a weighting of at least 80% and for modular schemes, where some examinations may be taken throughout the period of the course, it is 50%. For example, the Northern Examinations and Assessment Board (NEAB) offers two Mathematics Syllabuses:

Syllabus A: 80% Terminal examination (two papers covering Ma 2,3,4),
                  20% coursework (Ma1).
Syllabus B: 100% Terminal examination (two papers covering Ma 2,3,4;
                  one paper covering Ma 1).

The coursework should be integral to the course with a portfolio of work being drawn up over time. This portfolio can consist of tasks drawn up by the NEAB or devised by the school, and at the end of the course a minimum of two pieces of work is selected to support the final assessment. It is intended that over the tasks in the portfolio, attainment in the three strands of:

- making and monitoring decisions to solve problems
- communicating mathematically
- developing skills of mathematical reasoning

will be addressed.

For Syllabus A, the paper assessing Ma1 (1hour 30 mins in the foundation tier, 2 hours in the higher tier) will consist of two questions also designed to address the above three strands.

Either syllabus can also be delivered and assessed in smaller units, through the National Profile and Records of Achievement Scheme, whereby credits can be obtained as units are completed. These can accumulate towards a statement of achievement on the student's NPRA. There are other similar graduated assessment schemes, e.g. the Graduated Assessment Profile run by the School Mathematics Project, where credits accumulated can build up to a GCSE grade.

POST-16 QUALIFICATIONS

Many, but not all, student teachers will have gained their qualifications through 'A' levels and then degrees in Higher Education, but a significant number will have also attained vocational qualifications. Recently, there have been recommendations for a more unified national awards framework where equal status is given to academic, applied and vocational qualifications. For prospective mathematics teachers, the main impact of this will be the introduction of Key Skills courses in the Application of Number and the reform of 'AS/A' levels.

Key skills

The Application of Number will be one of the six categories of key skills integrated into the GNVQ (General National Vocational Qualification, which may be renamed as Applied 'A' level) and the NVQ (National Vocational Qualification) framework.

Examples of some of the aims are:

> . . . to enable candidates to
> 2.1 develop their mathematical knowledge and oral, written and practical skills in a manner which encourages confidence;
> 2.4 solve realistic problems, present the solutions clearly, check and interpret results;
> 2.10 develop their mathematical and IT capabilities by considering problems and conducting individual and cooperative enquiry and experiment, including pieces of work of a practical investigational kind.
>
> (NEAB, 1997)

Certificates will be awarded at three levels indicating progression in:

- Collecting and recording data.
- Tackling problems.
- Interpreting and representing data.

and the assessment, undertaken by a trained teacher and later moderated, is based on four units of work at each level. To complete a unit successfully the student must have achieved *every* specified outcome. For example, in a level 1 unit 'Using Shape, Space and Measures' the student will have to successfully achieve 10 outcomes including:

> 1. design and use a data collection sheet to show to a given degree of accuracy, the dimensions, weights of contents and prices of a specified sample of cuboidal boxes of a familiar product e.g. breakfast cereal, detergent;
> 2. convert between simple metric and imperial units of length;
> 3. classify the data and use simple fractions, decimals and percentages to describe the distributions.
>
> (NEAB, 1997)

AS/A levels

In line with the general Conservative move towards centralised control of the curriculum, the government, through SCAA, have stipulated a core of knowledge, understanding, skills and assessment objectives common to all GCE 'A' and 'AS' syllabuses in Mathematics. This has been pushed through very quickly and has been a controversial move since the consultative consisted largely of academics (who have as yet a free reign over their own courses) and examiners, with little teacher involvement (Neumark, 1997).

Some of the main changes are

- the 'AS' – Advanced Subsidiary – now becomes the first half of an 'A' level;
- core content including work on mathematical notions of proof;
- at least 25% of teaching time to be spent on one application of mathematics;
- at least 25% of the overall award to be assessed by an element in which candidates are not permitted to use a calculator or a computer;

- the inclusion of extended questions rather than graded or 'stepped' problems;
- a list of formulae which have to be remembered.

At the present time, there are both linear courses assessed by terminal examinations and modular courses taken by 20% of candidates. Some of the regulations for these modular courses have been tightened up:

- two examination sittings a year
- resits limited to one per module
- four or six modules in each subject (two or three for 'AS')
- at least 30% to be assessed terminally, of which half will be drawn from all areas of the course (a synoptic element).

By the year 2000, all courses will be available in modular form, and their increasing popularity is expected to continue.

CONCLUSIONS

It is very clear that the whole of the curriculum and qualifications framework in England and Wales has undergone a period of immense upheaval since the mid-1980s, and that this has had an enormous impact upon the work of schools and colleges. Never before has the educational system been bombarded with such a mass of policy initiatives. There are many contradictions in all of this – the rhetoric of equipping school leavers for life and work in the twenty first century, and yet the return to methods which pre-date the age of information technology, the centralisation of control in the hands of government agencies and yet the increased autonomy offered to schools in controlling their budgets and intake, the notion of equal opportunities alongside the humiliation of schools with the use of raw data in league tables.

In mathematics, these contradictions and inconsistencies are also present. How do we acknowledge the enormous impact of technology without losing other cherished aspects of mathematics? How do we popularise the subject and maintain challenge for high attainers? How do we help students to apply their knowledge in problem-solving situations and help them to develop sound conceptual structures at the same time? How can we hold on to the experience of mathematics as a creative, and fascinating study alongside the relentless drive for competitiveness and relevance? These are just some of the questions which new teachers will have to grapple with throughout their working lives.

REFERENCES

Department of Education and Science and the Welsh Office (1987) *National Curriculum Task Group on Assessment and Testing, A Report*. London: HMSO.

Department of Education and Science and the Welsh Office (1989) *Mathematics in the National Curriculum*. London: HMSO.

Department of Education and Science (1991) *Mathematics in the National Curriculum*. London: HMSO.

Department for Education (1995) *Mathematics in the National Curriculum*. London: HMSO.

National Curriculum Council (1989) *Mathematics: Non-Statutory Guidance*. York: NCC.

Neumark, V. (1997) 'The route to rigorous reasoning', in Extra Mathematics, *The Times Educational Supplement*, 21 March, II.

Northern Examination and Assessment Board (1997) *Certificate in Key Skills, Syllabus for 1997 & 1998, Application of Number, 6901*.

School Curriculum and Assessment Authority (1995a) *GCSE Regulations and Criteria*. London: SCAA.

School Curriculum and Assessment Authority (1995b) *GCSE Mandatory Code of Practice*. London: SCAA.

School Curriculum and Assessment Authority (1996a) *Key Stage 3 Assessment Arrangements*. London: SCAA.

School Curriculum and Assessment Authority (1996b) *Report on the 1995 Key Stage 2 Tests and Tasks in English, Mathematics and Science*. London: SCAA.

School Curriculum and Assessment Authority (1997) *Standards at Key Stage 3, Mathematics, Report on the 1996 National Curriculum Assessments for 14 -year-olds*. London: SCAA.

2: Why do I want to be a mathematics teacher?

APPLICATIONS

The students who start on a course of initial training have increasingly varied backgrounds and their motivation for entering teaching range from the idealistic to the practical need to get a job in a depressed economy. It is also becoming more common for entrants to have some knowledge of teaching already, from voluntary work in schools, involvement with sports coaching, experience of training in industry or in the informal setting of the home where parents participate in their children's learning from an early age.

When applying for the course and stating their reasons for wanting to teach, students clearly have an eye to the degree of honesty they can sensibly allow in an application form. The statements therefore make interesting reading. Redundancy and the pressing need to get a job are sometimes stated:

> 'I am now unemployed and feel I should take this opportunity to become a teacher and fulfil an ambition.'

> 'I enjoyed teaching in . . . and now need a formal qualification so that I can teach in the UK.'

but applicants are sometimes understandably reticent about their practical motivation. They may not realise that pragmatic reasons are perfectly valid and understood, as long as there are other reasons to support an informed choice.

Many of the applicants refer to their attraction to the profession because of its perceived importance. These stress the importance of schooling to individuals and to society as a whole:

> 'I feel that education is a very important factor in helping people to make choices and to fulfil their potential. I would enjoy the challenge of helping young people to reach their goals.'

> 'I would like to use my knowledge and experience in a socially constructive way.'

Balancing such worthy aims is the legitimate desire to find enjoyment and pleasure in the profession:

'I feel that teaching is a very exciting and progressive profession, where no two days would be the same.'

'For the last 3 years, teaching is all I have ever wanted to do. During this period, I have experienced how satisfying helping children can be.'

Another very popular theme in these personal statements involves the productive use of the applicant's skills and qualities:

'I have found that I relate well to children of all ages, but secondary school age in particular.'

'I am patient, kind, fair, calm and hard working and over the years have developed organisational, administrative, and presentational skills, all of which I would like to put to use.'

Almost all refer to their desire to teach mathematics, and it is here that some of the statements reveal strong beliefs about the teaching and learning of mathematics. Clearly the applicants are successful at mathematics, and they want to help children to share their understandings:

'I would enjoy passing on the knowledge and skills I have acquired during my education.'

'I helped . . . with GCSE mathematics . . . and I could explain the theory to them in a way they could understand.'

'My desire to teach began in my fifth year of secondary school, where I took great pleasure in communicating complicated ideas to my friends . . . I enjoyed thinking of new ways to explain things . . . My recent research [on an undergraduate course on children's learning of mathematics] has provoked more interest in me.'

'I believe I can make the learning process of what some consider "difficult" subjects more attractive to students and instigate and maintain their interest.'

At this stage in the course, it would seem then that teaching mathematics is a matter of explaining, communicating and passing on mathematical knowledge from teacher to learner. During the course of the year, students may come to realise that teaching mathematics also involves finding out and building upon what pupils already know, helping pupils to construct their own understandings and even learning mathematics from the pupils themselves. This is a profound shift in conceptualisation which some students, for a variety of reasons, reject or fail to make in their first year of training. Others are only just beginning to engage with this important reorientation, and will need further professional support in order to develop their teaching strategies to reflect this change of emphasis from teaching to learning.

Many applicants claim to be enthusiastic about mathematics as a subject, but it is not clear how much of this is due to the fact that they can do it and how much is due to a deeply felt curiosity and interest in the subject for its own sake. Moreover, since mathematics is generally felt to be a useful and even difficult subject, this enthusiasm may owe more to a feeling of being special and successful than anything else.

'I have a genuine interest in mathematics.'

'I have always been enthusiastic about mathematics.'

'I would also like to pass on my enthusiasm to others.'

One of the things which students such as these may find difficult may be in questioning their taken for granted assumptions that mathematics is enjoyable and that it is necessarily useful. They may never have wanted to question why they were learning particular mathematical techniques or concepts, because success has been a sufficient motivator.

THE INTERVIEW

At interview, I frequently ask students to explain a mathematical 'sum' like 0.2 multiplied by 0.3 , or 6 divided by 3/4 or to explain what a sine is. These apparently straightforward items from the conventional mathematics curriculum are often difficult for students to explain without resorting to rote rules, but even more difficult for them is saying why pupils may need to learn these items. Almost all applicants think it is important that they should be on the curriculum, but applications and contexts for the sums usually prove very difficult or are excessively contrived. For example, a context for the first question given by an inventive applicant was 'Five children buy a chocolate bar for 30p, how much will each share cost?'

This interview challenge is usually an eye opener for people who cite the relevance of mathematics for everyday life as a legitimate justification for teaching the subject. The reason for giving these questions at interview is not sadism. I want to prepare students for the questions that pupils will ask every day in the classroom, even if only to themselves, and to alert them to the need to provide justifications for those pupils but also for themselves. A career spent teaching concepts and techniques which are legitimised by others will not be fulfilling or exciting. Learning mathematical items because they are in the National Curriculum and will help pupils to pass exams are rather one-dimensional reasons and will not satisfy all pupils, particularly those of an independent and questioning bent. The paradox is that these reasons may have been enough for our prospective teachers and they may dry up in the face of the question 'What's the point of learning this?'

Without detracting in any way from the genuine motives and positive attitudes of these students, it needs to be recognised that over the course of a busy, demanding and sometimes difficult year, early idealism may take a battering. There will be uncomfortable lessons to learn about the self, schools, peers, pupils and teachers. The students' own enthusiasm for mathematics may decline in the face of apathetic pupils on a Friday afternoon, confidence in the ability to explain may be dented by the blank faces of incomprehension which stare back across the classroom, and the desire to help pupils fulfil their potential may dim when the curriculum on offer holds no delights for the learners.

There will be good times too, when pupils grasp new ideas, retain understandings or surprise the students with their insights and strategies. It will be difficult not to take either of these personally, and to accept that failure may be due to factors outside the student's control and that success may be the happy coincidence of the class teacher's support, a well-motivated group of successful pupils and good departmental resources. In my experience, many students, particularly females, are more ready to accept personal responsibility for disappointments than they are to accept congratulations for success. This modesty is laudable but there are times when it is important to recognise and note achievements, and celebrate them.

In teaching mathematics, one particular feature of the training year may be the way in which students begin to experience the intellectual challenge of learning about learning, as opposed to the intellectual challenge of solving mathematics problems. Students who would really rather be doing the mathematics than helping pupils to learn are out of place in the profession – it is not a refuge for frustrated mathematicians.

It is enormously helpful, however, to continue doing challenging mathematical problems and exploring mathematics for its own sake alongside teaching, and I would encourage teachers to try to do this throughout their careers. The benefits of this are two-fold. Clearly a wide and deep knowledge of mathematics is enriching and enables the teacher to flesh out what may be a very partial view of the subject, even if it has been pursued to degree level. Secondly, and this may be the more important reason, it gives the teacher an opportunity to feel what it is like to be a learner again, to experience the flashes of understanding and the state of being stuck, to realise that solutions may be arrived at in a messy and disorganised fashion, and that they frequently need rewriting and refining if someone else is to understand them. If this is done both individually and in a group, the teacher may become aware of the moments when they gain from other people's ideas, and when they are confused by lots of voices all talking at once, when they need a helping hand, and when they need to be by themselves.

This model of drawing out teaching implications from the student's own working on mathematical problems is very commonly used on training and in-service teaching, but the transference to the classroom is not always automatic. A very explicit consideration of possible implications is needed, which can then feed into practical strategies for the classroom.

TIME LINES

All students on a teacher training course bring with them educational histories which may influence their beliefs about mathematics, how it is learned and how it is taught. Reflecting and sharing these is a useful way of bringing assumptions to the surface and realising that there are a multiplicity of experiences, even though the group of trainee teachers is distinctive in having been successful, but perhaps not uniformly, in their mathematical careers. One way to do this is to draw a time line, marking

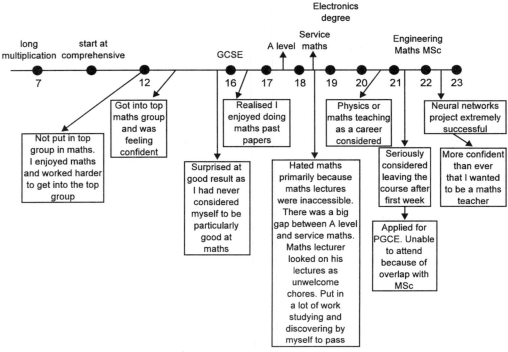

Figure 2.1   Martin's time line

important events along the way, with official landmarks marked on one side of the line and more personal 'critical incidents' on the other (Figures 2.1 and 2.2).

Discussion can flesh out these incidents and some patterns may emerge. It is very common for success or failure in examinations and work experience to feature on the official side, whereas critical incidents tend to feature relationships with family, peers or teachers, positive and negative feelings, and features of learning situations in which the individuals have been involved. There are also some very personal and idiosyncratic incidents which none the less have been memorable incidents for the student.

For one teacher, an unofficial critical incident occurred during an examination in the fourth year of secondary education:

'I can remember it vividly. The two classrooms were usually partitioned with large glass and polished wood screens, and these were thrown back to make space for the termly exams. Up to then I had been a high achiever, but I was good across the board in all subjects and did not feel particularly drawn to mathematics. But this exam was exciting – there is no other word for it. All the isolated topics we had been learning seemed to have been thrown together in a giant jigsaw puzzle and it was fun trying to figure it all out. When I walked for the bus with my friends it was clear that they had found it very difficult and were quite upset. This surprised me because they were all very bright but it probably added to my sense of achievement. If I had been in a larger school,

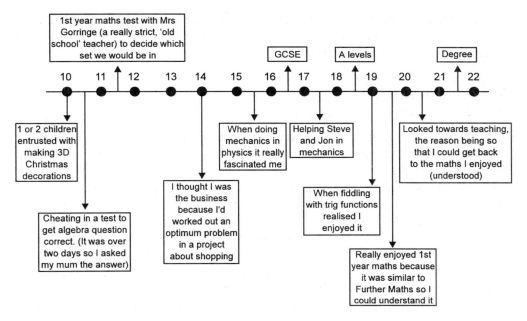

Figure 2.2 Alison's time line

there may have been more girls like me, but I was on my own in that class – maybe feeling special and successful added to my enjoyment of mathematics, and set me on a mathematical track for life.'

It is interesting that in this case, it is not the influence of a particularly good teacher which was important, but the activity of doing mathematics itself. Other students and teachers can identify personal influences, however, and in the biographical accounts of primary students collected by John Crook and Mary Briggs (1991) these featured prominently.

Negative experiences are not uncommon:

'In my second year at University, I really lost my way. Having been very focused I started to question what the mathematics was all about. It seemed unbelievably abstract, which may not have worried me too much if I hadn't started to have genuine difficulty with it. I think you can suspend feelings of irrelevance if you are successful. Well I didn't do much work and I actually failed one of the papers at the end of the year which was a real shock to me. Next year I worked hard and regained my zest – largely because I was determined to get at least a 2:1 but also because some of the units were very interesting, e.g. axiomatic set theory! And I also had a lecturer who took an interest in us as learners and actually set up situations where we discussed the work etc. I met him many years later and he said that the course he had taught had been new and was much too difficult for undergraduates so they had modified it the next year. That was a real eye opener for me – I hadn't realised that the courses were changed from year to year. I thought it was all set in tablets of stone.'

Although these incidents were all retold by successful mathematicians, it is clear that they have had their share of poor teaching and negative learning experiences. Common threads in the accounts were:

- the feeling of being good at mathematics
- enjoyment in doing mathematics
- increasing lack of understanding with mathematics at University.

Evidently the good experiences have outweighed the bad and the desire to teach must be accompanied by a willingness to help pupils along a sometimes challenging path, despite the difficulties.

Looking back over one's past learning can unearth valuable material upon which the student teacher can begin to work. Research (Petty and Hogben, 1980) confirms the view that student teachers already have strong images of teachers and teaching before they enter a course of teacher education, and that some of the attempts which teacher educators make to develop, reform or even change these perceptions may be very unsuccessful. With practising teachers, Tripp (1993) uses the device of examining critical incidents so that they should begin to question what they take for granted, examine their practice and begin to alter their usual approaches with a view to changing and improving them. So the time lines are not just interesting in tracing the individual's route into the profession, they may be a way of encouraging self-examination. This does require some willingness on the part of the student and later the teacher, to consider changing the status quo, and the presence of a critical friend to give support but also to ask some difficult questions.

REFERENCES

Crook, J. and Briggs, M. (1991) 'Bags and baggage', in *Teaching and Learning School Mathematics*. D. Pimm and E. Love (eds). London: Hodder and Stoughton.

Petty, M. and Hogben, D. (1980) 'Explorations of semantic space with beginning teachers: a study of socialization into teaching', *British Journal of Teacher Education*, **6**, 51–61.

Tripp, D. (1993) *Critical Incidents in Teaching: Developing Professional Judgement*. London: Routledge.

3: What does higher education offer?

RATIONALE FOR THE COURSE

The design and delivery of a course of teacher education will undoubtedly be influenced by the educational philosophy of the tutors both in the IHE and the partnership schools, but these courses have been closely regulated by government bodies for well over a decade now, and are inspected to ensure that they comply with government policy. So the media image of trendy educationists peddling a host of unworkable theories is completely inaccurate.

DfE Circular 9/92 (Figure 3.1) not only ushered in school based training, it brought with it a new concept in educating student teachers. This was a shift from previous courses in which the content had been carefully scrutinised by the Council for Accreditation of Teacher Education, to assessment led courses, in which students have to demonstrate specified competencies. This amounts to specifying what a competent teacher should be able to do in order to be offered qualified teacher status. At the time of writing, however, this framework is being changed again and the new focus is upon standards required of newly qualified teachers.

The examples used in this book are all from students following a competence-based course, in which the legislation has been interpreted in an individual but not unusual way. To my knowledge, no institution has taken the assessment of competence to its logical conclusion and passed students when they have successfully demonstrated competence, whether the year's course is completed or not. Most have used the competence list as a framework around which to plan a HE based programme, practical teaching, training in school and assessed work, and the whole package is designed to give students the opportunity to demonstrate their competence in a variety of ways. In assessing students, both the school and the HE tutors have to exercise judgements based upon evidence but inevitably taking into account some contextual factors.

For instance, all students are required to 'demonstrate an ability to select and use appropriate resources such as information technology' (2.3.7). Here IT is recognised as a resource alongside others such as structural apparatus, measuring equipment and text books. Clearly the opportunities to show competence with IT vary across schools, but at the very least students will be expected to be able to plan and execute lessons in which calculators are used appropriately and to have some successful experience of using computers with pupils learning mathematics. This competence

DFE Circular No. 9/92
Annex A (abstract)

1. Aim of Initial teacher training

1.1 All newly qualified teachers entering maintained schools should have achieved the levels of knowledge and standards of professional competence necessary to maintain and improve standards in schools.

1.2 The planning and management of training courses should be the shared responsibility of higher education institutions and schools in partnership.

2. Competences expected of newly qualified teachers

2.1 Higher education institutions, schools and students should focus on the competences of teaching throughout the whole period of initial training. The progressive developments of these competences should be monitored regularly during initial training. Their attainment at a level appropriate to newly qualified teachers should be the objective of every student taking a course of initial training.

Subject Knowledge

2.2 Newly qualified teachers should be able to demonstrate:

2.2.1 an understanding of the knowledge, concepts and skills of their specialist subjects and of the place of these subjects in the school curriculum;

2.2.2 knowledge and understanding of the National Curriculum and attainment targets (NCATS) and the programmes of study (PoS) in the subjects they are preparing to teach, together with an understanding of the framework of the statutory requirements;

2.2.3 a breadth and depth of subject knowledge extending beyond PoS and examination syllabuses in school.

Subject Application

2.3 Newly qualified teachers should be able to:

2.3.1 produce coherent lesson plans which take account of NCATs and of the school's curriculum policies;

2.3.2 ensure continuity and progression within and between classes and in subjects;

2.3.3 set appropriately demanding expectations for pupils;

2.3.4 employ a range of teaching strategies appropriate to the age, ability and attainment level of pupils;

2.3.5 present subject content in clear language and in a stimulating manner;

2.3.6 contribute to the development of pupil's language and communication skills;

2.3.7 demonstrate an ability to select and use appropriate resources including information technology.

Class Management

2.4 Newly qualified teachers should be able to:

2.4.1 decide when teaching the whole class, groups, pairs, or individuals is appropriate for particular learning purposes.

2.4.2 create and maintain a purposeful and orderly environment for the pupils;

2.4.3 devise and use appropriate rewards and sanctions to maintain an effective learning environment;

2.4.4 maintain pupils' interest and motivation.

Assessment and Recording of Pupils' Progress

2.5 Newly qualified teachers should be able to:

2.5.1 identify the current level of attainment of individual pupils using NCATS, statements of attainment and end of key stage statements where applicable;

2.5.2 judge how well each pupil performs against the standard expected of a pupil of that age;

2.5.3 assess and record systematically the progress of individual pupils;

2.5.4 use such assessments in their teaching;

2.5.5 demonstrate that they understand the importance of reporting to pupils on their progress and of marking their work regularly against agreed criteria.

Further Professional Developments

2.6 Newly qualified teachers should have acquired in initial training the necessary foundation to develop:

2.6.1 an understanding of the school as an institution and its place within the community;

2.6.2 a working knowledge of their pastoral, contractual, legal and administrative responsibilities as teachers;

2.6.3 an ability to develop effective working relationships with professional colleagues and parents, and to develop their communication skills;

2.6.4 an awareness of individual differences, including social, psychological, developmental and cultural dimensions;

2.6.5 the ability to recognise diversity of talent including that of gifted pupils;

2.6.6 the ability to identify special educational needs or learning difficulties;

2.6.7 a self-critical approach to diagnosing and evaluating pupils' learning, including a recognition of the effects on that learning of teachers' expectations;

2.6.8 a readiness to promote the moral and spiritual well-being of pupils.

Figure 3.1

may be demonstrated in the classroom but it may also be evident in assignments, where students may produce lesson activities involving a wide range of potential resources. It could also be assessed in a school-based project, when students can explore an area in which they have not had sufficient experience.

The final group of competencies feel different from the earlier ones which concentrate largely upon teaching performance, but it would be a mistake to think that they are not relevant in the mathematics classroom. For instance, an interpretation of success in '[having] the necessary foundation to develop . . . an awareness of individual differences, including social, psychological, developmental and cultural dimensions' would be the students' use of strategies to encourage the equal participation of both boys and girls in all class activities, the choice of contexts appropriate to the age, interests and background of the pupils, and an awareness of how to handle pupils who lack confidence in learning mathematics.

STRUCTURE OF THE COURSE

Most courses are structured in a developmental way so that increasing demands are met progressively throughout the course. For instance, the structure of the course with which I am involved is:

Term 1:
- Primary school experience (2 weeks)
- IHE based with school based days (7 weeks)
- Diagnostic practice (1 week preparation + 4 weeks practice).

Term 2:
- IHE based week
- IHE based with school based days (n weeks)
- Main practice (first phase)

Term 3:
- Main practice (second phase)
- IHE based week
- School based project
- Further professional development

For mathematics students, common critical hurdles of the year are:

- The first written assignment, especially when it is some time since an essay has been written.
- The first lesson alone with a class.
- The first written feedback.
- Visit from the HE tutor.
- School reports at the end of practices.

The emphasis on the assessment of teaching practice elements in this list is not surprising. Not only do students see teaching experience as crucial – it is the most widely studied aspect of Teacher Education courses (Feiman-Nemser, 1983). There is a danger, then, of seeing the written assignments as hurdles to be overcome rather than important opportunities to research and reflect upon teaching and learning mathematics. These assignments are not intended to be dry academic exercises, and frequently ask students to integrate work with pupils within a framework informed by reading and reflection. Some examples of the mathematics assignments done in the first half of the course illustrate this point.

EXAMPLES OF WRITTEN MATHEMATICS ASSIGNMENTS

Assignment 1

Students working in groups research two mathematical topics from the school curriculum focusing upon:

(a) Why pupils should learn these topics.
(b) The key ideas and progression within the topic.
(c) Different approaches, including practical applications, problem solving, investigational work and the use of IT.
(d) Pupils' responses to the topic, including aspects which they find difficult, or evidence of their own methods, informed by work with pupils and/or discussions with teachers.

The students then do presentations with follow-up discussion and the submitted assignment consists of:

1. An overview of the two topics including points raised in the presentation discussion.
2. An evaluation of the students' own learning as a result of the activity.

This assignment is deliberately placed first and the topics chosen for their ubiquity, e.g. directed numbers, angles, equations, 3D shapes. It gives the students valuable opportunities to find out and share different ways of teaching common topics. For Shulman and Grossman (1988) this *pedagogical content knowledge* is one of the seven domains of a teacher's knowledge and includes:

> the most powerful analogies, illustrations, examples, explanations and demonstrations – in a word the ways of representing the subject which makes it comprehensible to others . . . [It] also includes an understanding of what makes the learning of specific topics easy or difficult . . . (Shulman, 1986).

This is an aspect which many students find difficult and which they struggle to develop over their training so it makes sense to tackle this early in the course and to disseminate the research as widely amongst the group as possible. Evaluations suggest that it is highly valued, and students certainly draw from this activity when planning lessons in any of the specific topics. It is deliberately designed to start with content areas and to integrate teaching approaches within them, since this is the way the vast majority of schools operate, and students therefore feel that this work is both relevant and useful to them. By requiring the presentations to be interactive and encouraging the researching students to dig deep in their research, an implicit strand is that some students may actually strengthen their own content knowledge in the process. This is an aspect which has been found to be lacking in prospective teachers in the USA:

> . . . their knowledge of mathematics is not sufficiently connected to enable them to break away from the common approach to teaching and learning mathematics by compartmentalising topics.
>
> (Brown, 1992; referring to research by Ball, 1990a, b)

and is reinforced by some of the comments students have made in the self-evaluation part of this assignment:

> 'This assignment has enabled me to see that a lot of topics can be related, e.g. fractions, probability, ratios.'

At first sight this may seem alarming, coming from a graduate student, but what is being revealed here is an explicit awareness of connectedness. I have no doubt that the student has successfully used the links between these topics to solve problems in the past and has switched effortlessly between them but he has never been fully aware of the relationships. Hopefully, being aware of these connections will be a first step in helping pupils to make them.

In other comments, it is encouraging to find that some students are not just thinking about the topics and the possible teaching approaches in the abstract, but beginning to think of the pupils' perspective:

> '. . . Now, as adults, we have developed strategies for coping with mathematical problems. Teaching is not just a case of thinking how we would understand the subject being explained. Children have to develop "mental muscles" and acquire techniques, such as abstract thought, just as the body has to develop before certain athletic feats can be attempted.'

and of how decisions will still need to be made in different contexts:

> 'I have learnt an awful lot about ways to approach both topics. I will now have to spend some time reflecting on how to fit these ideas into lessons, and how to adapt them to different situations.'

Even at this early stage in the course, there is an opportunity to link the library work with what students are finding in their own as yet limited experience of teaching. Again, this is a deliberate feature of the design, as is the recommendation that students discuss their research and findings with practising teachers. Not only will some of these teachers be able to offer students the benefit of their knowledge gained by experience with pupils, it may also be an opportunity for the student teacher to offer some insights to the practising teachers, whether from the reading or from observing pupils closely:

> 'Our research into this subject [directed numbers] has certainly made me appreciate how much more difficult a subject this is to teach than it at first appears. This first introduction to abstract thinking is likely to shape the child's whole mathematical future so that great care must be taken when planning its introduction. Of the teachers that we talked to about this subject, many favour scrapping the number line concept and introduce integers in general as discrete values. Yet surely this will lead to problems later in pupils' mathematical education when rational and irrational numbers are introduced to complete that same number line. I favour a mixed introduction – allowing pupils to see negative numbers as an extension of the natural numbers and to explore them first in context and then more abstractly, using the number line as necessary.'

Assignment 2

This is a report of pupils learning how to use and apply mathematics in which the students need to provide:

1. a rationale for pupils using and applying mathematics;
2. an interpretative report of one or two activities done with a small group of pupils, using a video to help with the analysis; and
3. an evaluation in terms of the initial rationale and in terms of self-learning.

This is meant to be a more demanding activity than the first one, since it involves the students in planning and teaching in a way that is probably unfamiliar to them and uncommon in many of their schools. Moreover, the students are now responsible for planning and teaching their own material, and the use of the video gives them an opportunity to revisit the experience. Students generally find the use of the video threatening, but once they have overcome their apprehension many of them find it a useful experience. The assignment itself is couched in the language of the National Curriculum which has an assessable section of the mathematics curriculum devoted to problem solving, communicating mathematics and mathematical reasoning, so the focus can be legitimised, but students do find this approach more controversial than the content led approach of the previous assignment. Again, the timing and design is deliberate and the aim that teachers in school and students may learn from each other is real.

The really important purpose behind this task is to give students an opportunity to think aloud about planning, teaching and evaluating an approach, not a topic. It is a chance for students to see how a certain way of working lives up to expectations, and to show that they can interpret the pupils' reactions to the activity. It does not matter for the purposes of the assignment if the lesson is not a great success – it is the way in which the student can account for difficulties and suggest improvements for the future that is important. The really valuable part is the account of what the student has learned from the experience. At one level, it is the evaluation of the approach which is under scrutiny:

> 'Although I didn't hold the extreme view that investigational/problem-solving was a "bolt-on" extra to the curriculum, I wasn't entirely comfortable with the idea that its application could support the other three attainment targets. I am now convinced that the wide and varied classification of problems and the broad range of support material available can mean that problem-solving can play a vital part in classroom activities.'

but comments of this kind are relatively rare. Much more usual are the comments which refer to the amount of structure within the task and how this could be changed:

> 'Before I worked through the exercise with the pupils, I was confident that I was presenting a problem solving investigation . . . the investigation was not, however, as open ended as it first appeared. The aim was predetermined as was the pre-printed results sheet . . . [in future] I would begin with the definition and explanation about tessellations and pentominoes, and then I would present the resources and ask them how we could find out whether pentominoes tessellate. This question would then be open to discussion. The pupils would also have their own opportunity to design their own results table.'

Also common are observations about the role of the teacher:

> 'Basically because I took over the investigation the whole exercise was futile . . . '

> 'The difficulty with this kind of exercise . . . is when do you stop helping, stand back and let them go on with the investigation themselves.'

and the tension between maintaining an orderly classroom and fulfilling the aims of the activity:

> 'At the time of recording I had thought that some members of the group were off task and noisy . . . . However, with the aid of the video I have since concluded that the behaviour . . . wasn't as bad as it appeared at the time; moreover this behaviour may have been the result of allowing them to work in pairs for the first time . . . .'

One student's comments seem to sum up many of these tensions:

> 'In terms of the initial justification the activity was not successful. This was because:
>
> (1) none of the pupils came close to deriving Pict's theorem
> (2) the area of the shapes was calculated using method i and there was very little evidence of pupils using method ii
> (3) little original thought was evident.'

Here the student had a very clear idea of the result to be achieved and the method he was hoping the pupils would use and yet he also wanted the pupils to be original. He seems to have fallen between the two stools, and at this stage his strategies for the future are hazy.

Assignment 3

In this piece, groups of students produce a taped discussion of a theme in mathematics education, based on selected readings from journal articles.

Here the assignment is intended to raise the students' awareness of wider issues, e.g. equal opportunities, ability and attainment, attitudes and motivation. Apart from the obvious aim of encouraging students to explore some of these constructs in depth, the secondary aims of having to work as a team and to do some library searches of unfamiliar territory are also important. Taping the discussion as an alternative to the written submission offers the students a chance to work interactively. It also seems to give me a closer insight into their understandings since they are having to explain arguments and sometimes defend a position to the others. In some of the discussions the group have been able to move their own thinking along, by reflecting critically on the articles, and finding personal implications. For instance, one group who had researched the theme of misconceptions had a very useful exchange about the misconceptions exposed by their articles, and then went on to give examples from their own teaching practice:

- the smaller from larger error in the standard algorithm for subtraction

  34
  −17
  ──
  23
- not having percentages larger than 100%
- area is length 'times' breadth, irrespective of the shape

As the groups became more relaxed and they were discussing understanding in general, one student's challenge provoked an illuminating exchange:

> S1: Does anyone understand properly why when you divide by a fraction, you turn it upside down and multiply . . . (mutterings of 'no' from the rest) . . . I suppose I should have sat down and tried to work that out for myself.
>
> S2: We'll have to get Maria to explain it to us . . . That's the thing, if we don't understand it how can we teach the kids in a way that we try to avoid any further misconceptions. That's our quandary isn't it?

This demonstrated well an awareness of shallow understanding, but a lack of confidence in their own ability to sort it out, and a general anxiety about future teaching. I was able to raise this point with them and stress the need for them to continue looking for explanations and analogies to use in their teaching, but also to consider the strategy of returning to justifications and explanations in a cyclical fashion over time (Johnson *et al.*, 1989).

For those readers who do not understand the division rule for fractions themselves here are a few clues which could be developed into a generalisable explanation:

- 10 divided by 2/3 *means* 'how many 2/3 s are in 10?'

There are three thirds in each interval – so how many thirds in 10?
How would you find out how many 2/3 s in 10?

THE ROLE OF HIGHER EDUCATION

> Universities ought to be places of research, scholarship and critical though informed deliberation. Such deliberation need not be immediately practical, but indirectly it must be so that any practice participates in a world of ideas and is affected by the shifts and changes within that world of ideas . . . .
>
> . . . For schools to be centres in which trainee teachers become professionals, intelligently exploring the ideas beneath the practices which are being introduced, rather than blindly apprenticed to existing practice . . . they need to be plugged in to a wider network of intellectual life where critical enquiry, deliberation, questioning, speculation and research are central rather than peripheral activities. Universities at their best provide the framework and the stimulus for such a framework.
>
> (Pring, R. 1996)

The intellectual challenge of learning about learning may come as a relief to some students after concentrating upon the mathematics in their undergraduate degree, but the degree of reflection required may be dismissed by those who see teaching as an essentially practical and untheorised affair. The division between schools and universities is less stark now that partnerships have been developed and that tutors have clearly delineated roles and responsibilities. For instance, it is very common for students to spend time in structured observation, records of which are taken back into the IHE to feed into group discussions. The idea is that the HE tutor can help the students to pool their observations and experiences, to analyse for similarities and differences and to test their emerging understandings against background reading. This process is often called the linking of theory and practice and lies behind the design of the written assignments already discussed in this chapter.

Students training to teach mathematics need to appreciate the many meanings of the word theory. The word is often bandied about as if we all share a common understanding – the unfortunate fate of other words and phrases such as numeracy, the basics, discovery methods and many others. For some, theory is something you find in books, in IHE libraries, but not in schools. Another interpretation I have encountered amongst students is that of an ideal model, an aspiration which is forever out of reach, as in the phrase: 'Well, that's the theory, but it won't work in our school'.

The framework of the National Curriculum Mathematics orders could be taken as a theory if we adopt this interpretation. It is a model of the curriculum and its assessment, giving teachers the mathematical topics to be covered over the period of compulsory schooling, with an implied progression, but no statutory teaching methods. Other policy documents fall into this category, whether produced by the government at a national level or by the department in a school. Policies for special needs provision (Code of Practice), or for equal opportunities (School level), or for marking pupils' work are all examples. In professional preparation, teachers need to know about such policies, particularly those which are legally binding, and the IHE and school would be expected to provide such information throughout the year. It is also necessary, however, to examine policies critically for ideological bias or impracticability, and this is certainly a role for Higher Education.

A second interpretation of the word theory has links with scientific use. Here we are looking for explanations of natural phenomena, and to devise such theories we need to collect and interpret evidence systematically. In mathematics education, we have some excellent examples of such theories derived from the research of the last 10–15 years, e.g. the Concepts in Secondary Mathematics and Science project (Hart, 1981), the Strategies and Errors in Secondary Mathematics (e.g. Kerslake, 1986), and the Children's Mathematical Frameworks project (Johnson *et al.*, 1989). This research all deserves in-depth treatment, but a few findings can be summarised here:

- Many pupils fail to learn formal mathematical processes which they have been taught, and resort to restricted informal methods with which they feel comfortable.
- Many pupils have incomplete models of mathematical entities such as fractions.
- Some pupil errors are logical but are derived from faulty premises.

Some explanations put forward for these findings are that:

- Certain mathematical understandings take time to develop because they are intrinsically difficult.
- Teachers do not use a sufficiently wide range of models and language over time to help pupils develop sound understandings.
- Pupils are actively and systematically trying to make sense of the mathematics they encounter, and their errors may be a good starting point for future teaching.

Even though such work has been known and published for over a decade, many teachers have simply never encountered it, but the recent review, commissioned by OFSTED (Askew and Wiliam, 1995), goes some way to making this and other research more accessible. Interestingly, Dylan Wiliam suggests that the schools which have used this review more as a source of *questions* to stimulate discussion amongst staff than as a set of answers are better able to use the research to improve their own professional practice. In the training institution, students would be expected to engage in a similar practice – sharing observed practices and problems, and using guided reading of research to inform their reflections and later practice. It is an ongoing process, the seeds of which can be sown more easily in the IHE because of access to recorded research and the allocation of time for reflection and discussion.

Not all research is large scale, and not all research seeks to explain. There is a long-standing tradition of practitioner research, i.e. research done by teachers in their own classrooms. Close to the action, and sensitive to context, such research has the potential to inform practice with an immediacy denied to the big projects with their heavy research reports and problems of dissemination. The emphasis here is upon a better understanding of the teacher's classroom or school by disciplined enquiry.

Trainee teachers could encounter this sort of research if teachers in their schools are exploring significant issues for them as part of their study for a higher degree, but if not, the IHE will certainly have examples of such action research in the library. Ideally, of course, these different interpretations of theory should be mutually supportive. The small-scale action research which illuminates practice should complement large-scale projects which may have a greater emphasis upon explanations and generalisability, and we would all hope that educational policy would be informed by research evidence, not political whim or expedience.

Although I have concentrated on the role of the IHE in developing theory, I should return to the initial interpretation which suggested that theory is out of place in schools. This is an understandable but mistaken view. The teacher who says 'These children will never learn much, they mostly come from broken homes' is making a generalisable statement explaining academic performance in terms of family structure. The teacher who says 'Lee's method for doing subtraction works perfectly well and I'm not going to encourage him to change it' shows that he understands something of what Lee is doing in his head, and is adapting his teaching accordingly. The teacher who says 'Since I've had a student and we did that activity about questioning, I've been watching myself as I ask questions around the class and I've realised that I avoid asking that quiet group of boys at the side' is at the start of an enquiry which may develop into a systematic study of her personal teaching, resulting in some deliberate changes to her practice, which she may then start to evaluate.

All these aspects of theory are available for the student teacher to pursue in IHE based work, but there are other opportunities available for reading and reflection. I am referring to the wealth of curriculum development material available in professional journals such as Mathematics in Schools, Mathematics Teaching and Micromath. These are produced by the subject associations (the Mathematical Association and the Association of Teachers of Mathematics), one of which may have a branch locally, and contain collections of reflective writing, lesson accounts, ideas for classroom activities and evaluations of new resources. Not all of this represents systematic enquiry, and would not always count as research but it is well worth reading these journals since many of the articles are very accessible and represent a range of views from members of the mathematics education community.

ROLE OF THE IHE TUTOR

The inclusion of the written mathematics assignments earlier in this chapter attempt to illustrate how work at the IHE encourages deliberation and reflection in the subject area, usually as the responsibility of one or at most two mathematics curriculum tutors. In the move to school-based courses, the roles of these tutors have changed to incorporate more liaison with schools as well as their traditional roles with students. Whereas in the past '. . . the teachers in the school and the HE tutor [worked] largely in glorious isolation' (Gates, 1994), there is now a better footing for partnership. In principle, this should mean more dialogue and time for working together to achieve common aims both at a general and at a subject level, but in practice this is constrained by resources. For instance, in some partnerships, the HE mathematics tutor does not visit or observe the mathematics students in school, and has become a generic tutor attached to specific schools. In others, the mathematics tutor may observe the mathematics student teaching but providing feedback and support to the student may not be the primary aim here. She may be acting as a moderator to ensure that students across all the schools are having similar experiences and that assessment standards are as comparable as possible. Students interviewed were aware of these differences:

> '. . . they were looking for different things because the class teacher had observed me before and so was looking for a progression, this was the first time M . . . had seen me teach so for her it was more of a snapshot . . . '

> 'M . . . was interested in the curriculum, the way it was delivered, the pupils . . . what they learned making sure that I was aware of individual differences in the class, use of assessment in my teaching, in my use of examples. Whereas the classroom teacher was completely interested in the relationships with the pupils.'

> 'She must be a moderator, assessor for the course . . . a sort of pastoral role as well.'

The aim of course is for the HE tutor and the mathematics mentor in school to provide complementary roles which continue to develop with the partnerships. Both of them have a personal relationship with the student, but they are also working together to provide the right conditions for the student to develop. This does not mean that they will always be in agreement about what and how to teach, and tutors have to be particularly sensitive to the fact that students can feel torn between competing sets of expectations. Importantly, the HE tutor and the mathematics mentor may differ over whether the student should pass or fail, and this is where evidence must be carefully evaluated and other views brought in, initially those of other tutors and later of external examiners.

REFERENCES

Ball, D.L. (1990a) 'Prospective elementary and secondary teachers' understanding of division', *Journal for Research in Mathematics Education*, **21**, 132–44.

Ball, D.L. (1990b) 'The mathematical understandings that prospective teachers bring to teacher education', *Elementary School Journal*, **90**, 449–66.

Brown, C.A. (1992) 'Becoming a Mathematics teacher', in *Handbook of Research on Mathematics Teaching and Learning*, D.A. Grouws (ed.), 209–39. New York: Macmillan.

Department for Education (1992) *Initial Teacher Training (Secondary Phase)*, Circular 9/92. London: HMSO.

Feiman-Nemser, S. (1983) 'Learning to teach', in *Handbook on Teaching and Policy*, L. Shulman and G. Sykes (eds), 150–70. New York: Longman.

Gates, P. (1994) 'A focus on learning to teach', in *Mentoring in Mathematics Teaching*, B. Jaworski and A. Watson (eds), 13–28. London: Falmer.

Hart, K. (ed.) (1981) *Children's Understanding of Mathematics: 11–16*. London: John Murray.

Johnson, D. *et al.* (1989) *Children's Mathematical Frameworks*, 8–13. Berkshire: NFER-Nelson.

Kerslake, D. (1986) *Fractions: Children's Strategies and Errors*. Berkshire: NFER-Nelson.

Pring, R. (1996) 'Just desert', in *The Role of Higher Education in Initial Teacher Education*, J. Furlong and R. Smith (eds), 8–22. London: Kogan Page.

Shulman, L. (1986) 'Those who understand; knowledge growth in teaching', *Educational Researcher*, **15**, 4–14.

Shulman, L. and Grossman, P.L. (1988) *Knowledge Growth in Teaching*. A final report to the Spencer Foundation. Stanford, CA: Stanford University.

Part 2: In the Classroom

4: What will it feel like to be in school again?

EXPECTATIONS OF THE SCHOOL

In many ways, the role of the teaching practice schools is more obvious than that of the University. Here there are classes full of children to practice on, real teachers to provide role models and school structures and routines to provide stability and support. It would be naive to suggest, however, that the school practice is the straightforward part of the course or that consistency of experience can be guaranteed across schools. Whilst striving to provide comparable provision, there will inevitably be variation and this can be a strength particularly when students are placed in more than one school, as is common on many courses. In mathematics, for instance, a good contrast may be obtained by doing practice in a department which uses a commercial scheme such as the School Mathematics Project and in one where the department select from a variety of sources or produce their own.

Where the IHE takes responsibility for placements, there is always a certain amount of anxiety surrounding the allocation of students to schools. The publication of League Tables of examination results is one source of advance information, leading to the classification of schools by students into 'good', 'bad', 'nice' or 'rough'. Mathematicians should know the dangers of jumping to such conclusions on the basis of decontextualised data but they can still fall into this trap in the tense period before the first visit to their placement school. They need to remember that every school is different, that schools with reputations for academic excellence have their own pressures as well as schools struggling to provide for their pupils in unfavourable economic and social circumstances, and that the school's examination performance overall may not give a true picture of the department in which they will be working.

Another source of information about schools is the local reputation gleaned by those who have lived in an area for a length of time, and have perhaps compared schools as prospective parents. In several cases of my experience this knowledge has produced anxieties out of all proportion to the reality of the placements. In one case, a young local student suffered intolerable stress on behalf of her mother who felt that her daughter was going to be fed to the lions in a school with a local reputation for 'toughness'. The student faced up to the challenge, completed a very successful practice and took her first post in a similar school. She was of course supported and encouraged by a very professional team of mentors in the school, and learned a great deal about herself and teaching in the process.

Of course, starting a new school is not new to prospective student teachers as they have already experienced socialisation into a variety of institutions as learners. Clearly they will have learnt coping strategies from these previous experiences but now the extra dimension is that they will be learning and helping others to learn at the same time. Paradoxically, this first training year probably requires more adjustment to different settings and the requirement to perform within them as a teacher, albeit in a gradual way, than any other period in a teacher's professional career.

FIRST IMPRESSIONS

In the early stages of the course, when students are being introduced to their first school the desire to fit in with the ethos of the school and department may conflict with the early development of a personal philosophy of teaching. Written accounts reveal the importance of good first impressions:

'I [had begun] to formulate a very grim and raw idea of . . . comprehensive. When I arrived . . . I was greatly relieved for the comprehensive didn't even begin to resemble my dire mental image.'

and the need for a warm welcome from staff:

'I had initially felt apprehensive lest the department would see a PGCE student as a "burden" – but the time the staff spent to welcome M . . . and I, and to introduce and familiarise us to the department, dispelled such apprehension.'

but students are also exercising a critical eye:

'the head of department was very outgoing yet approachable and became a great source of help and information. Unfortunately his teaching style seemed a little strict, though well organised . . .'

'The last lesson of the day was the first that we observed. We were not introduced to the class, which I found rather strange. The class were in the top band and required little assistance which made the lesson uninteresting.'

'We were, however, told that such an impressive amount of materials shown on corridors was not normal and that this was mainly due to an up and coming Open Day.'

While taking in such impressions, students may also remember being at school themselves and start to think about how their role is now changing:

'As I walked down the corridor, I felt quite exhilarated to think I was there in the capacity of a potential teacher. As I got swamped in the tide of students (most of whom were taller than me!) at a lesson change I felt suddenly very small and vulnerable. I also felt very conspicuous in my non-school uniform.'

Although the student may feel like a split personality, it is important to realise that both accepting the practice in the school and wanting to be part of it, and being able to constructively criticise that practice is a healthy state. Being socialised into the department and school should not mean giving up one's personal philosophy and becoming sycophantic, although there will necessarily be some compromise on both sides. Socialisation need not be subjugation, rather a process of negotiation in which the student finds his or her own way of becoming a teacher within a ready-made but continually evolving context.

THE STRUCTURE OF SUPPORT

In the school, training will be the responsibility of designated staff, typically one in the mathematics department and one taking overall care of the mixed subject group of students in the school. These teachers will oversee routine organisational matters, and provide mentoring during the course of the practice, often in a timetabled slot. They may also arrange special training sessions on particular topics. Over the practice, students will probably see more of their mathematics mentor than the generic mentor, and they will hopefully come to realise the complexity of the role. At different times this mentor may be a role model as a teacher, a mediator between the student and other staff, a critical friend, an assessor and a counsellor – as well as a full-time teacher with other responsibilities in the department. In some courses, this person will take the sole responsibility for the school-based training and assessment of the mathematics teaching, since the IHE tutor with school links may not be a subject specialist. As mentioned previously, some HE institutions have been able to retain subject specialist tutors who may also visit and observe mathematics lessons, but they will almost certainly rely on the expertise and day-to-day knowledge of the subject mentor.

Students will also be supported by the teachers of the classes they are teaching, and it will be very common for these teachers to liaise with the departmental mentor. If this is done in an open and constructive way, support can be spread throughout the department, giving the student a range of different perspectives from which to learn.

There is an understandable tendency for students to identify with the mathematics department. There is a life outside the department, however, and the generic mentor will be able to give this wider perspective either personally or by arranging activities which involve the students in the wider life of the school. If this mentor observes a lesson, he or she may be able to give a critical perspective which may alert the students to aspects of teaching and learning which mathematicians in their shared world fail to notice. This can be very valuable.

COMPARISONS

Inevitably, students will be making comparisons between the teaching experience school and the schools(s) in which they were educated. For some, there may be very little difference but for others the differences may seem alarming. One student, educated in the private sector, admitted to being terrified of going to the comprehensive school in which she had been placed. For others, who were at school in the days of selection, when compulsory schooling ended at 15, the whole system has changed dramatically. If they have followed these changes as parents then the contrast will not seem so great, but even then it is unlikely that they will have had many experiences of sitting in on lessons and getting to know teachers as colleagues.

Comparisons will also be made about the teaching of mathematics. For many students, the use of an individualised learning scheme – such as the Kent Mathematics Project (KMP), SMILE (Secondary Mathematics Individualised Learning Experiment) or the booklets for Years 7 and 8 in the SMP scheme – is completely new. Several comments from mathematics students reveal difficulties in adjusting to this: 'I haven't done any proper teaching yet, just Kent lessons.'

Here they are revealing their own deep-seated beliefs about what constitutes teaching, and the idea of pupils working autonomously either individually or in small groups does not fit. There may also be some difficulty with the idea that learning can take place without a teacher around.

Another adjustment will be needed in seeing the full range of the school's pupils learning mathematics. Since many schools have sets in mathematics, the most familiar classrooms for most students will be the 'top' sets for older pupils. Here, both the content and level of the mathematics and the attitudes of the pupils may accord with their memories, and they may feel more at home in these classes. The sheer range of attainment and motivation across a whole school may be an eye opener, and the 'top' set may feel like a refuge. This is perfectly understandable, but students will have to recognise that their own school experience has been very partial and that they now need to widen their horizons if they are to be successful with all pupils.

Peter Gates (1994) warns against relying on memories of one's own schooling:

> First, we do not always remember as well as we think we do .... Second, each one of us has only limited access to the mind of one pupil (oneself) and no access to the minds of the teachers who taught us. Third, the new teacher was probably a successful pupil ... and is therefore unrepresentative .... Fourth ... the teaching methods one experienced may be limited in their wider application ....

So comparisons are unavoidable but have to be treated with caution. Students also need to remember that comparisons can be used for various defensive reasons, e.g. to distance oneself from a threatening situation, to assert superiority, etc. If it does all seem very unfamiliar, then comparing the experience with going on a holiday is a good way to think about it. Yes, there will be many unknowns, but these are opportunities to meet new people (teachers and pupils) with different but equally valid perspectives, to try new activities (teaching new topics in a different way), and to learn in the process.

As students begin to observe classes they will be making other comparisons, between the teachers they are watching and the teachers they want to be. This can be inspiring

'If I could ever be as good a teacher as RS I would be delighted.'

or dispiriting

'I sat in that lesson and I found it entrancing . . . and the kids still didn't really understand. I don't know if I could keep on trying like that – I think I'd just be ground down.'

If they are in a pair, then both the students and the teachers are bound to make comparisons between them. One female student who was paired with a very confident male student was completely thrown when he offered to teach a lesson at very short notice early in his observation period. She felt undue pressure to do the same herself even though she was not ready, and needed reassuring that she could take her own time. Her own analysis could not have been more apt: 'I mean, it's not a competition, is it?'

THE PROCESS OF SOCIALISATION

During the training year, students are becoming members of a professional culture. This is sometimes seen as the student being shaped by strong forces at school level but this view of the student's passivity is increasingly questioned. Certainly the structures and rhetoric of many training courses now imply the development of professional judgement which fits in more with a model of socialisation in which the student is a more active participant (Brown, 1992)) and this has been fleshed out empirically. In researching how ten mathematics students learned to establish themselves over their training year, Linda Haggerty (1995) used Lacey's (1977) classification of strategies:

- internalised adjustment
- strategic compliance
- strategic redefinition

to inform her analysis.

She found that, in coming to terms with their practice, some of them blamed either the management in the school or the pupils for any problems they experienced, although in discussion some of them came round to accepting their own inexperience as a contributory factor. In my experience some students also blame the IHE for not preparing them sufficiently. It was very rare for the students in Haggerty's study to accept the situation they were in, believing it was for the best (internalised adjustment) and most of them adopted the second strategy of conforming to the expectations of the authority figure, whilst harbouring private reservations. None of them managed to change the situation radically, since they had limited access to new ideas and had limited impact on the beliefs of the mentors with whom they were working, although being in the programme had this effect on the mentors. Linda's conclusions were that expecting the students to change and be changed radically was unrealistic, and that their learning could be hampered by the need to be polite with their mentors.

These insights are either depressing or realistic, depending on your perspective. On the one hand, it takes the pressure off student teachers to bring in new ideas and to implement them successfully in the classroom, without discouraging them from trying. On the other, it places an extra demand on HE tutors and mathematics mentors to find ways of opening up debate between students teachers and mentors in which disagreements can be aired in a constructive way.

WORKING WITH THE MENTOR

In my experience, many mathematics teachers have found the role of mentoring a fascinating and challenging new departure. Although their first priority will always be the progress of the pupils in their school, some of them have had to develop different skills in working with novice teachers who are still learners:

> When previously relationships with adults in the school had been based on friendship or collegiality, when assuming a mentoring role they need to be based more upon the need to create an effective learning environment for the student teacher.

(Gates, 1994)

Many students are only too willing to make themselves useful, and to get on with the business of teaching as soon as possible, and since there is always room for an extra pair of hands in the classroom there is a temptation to be seen as 'a real teacher' too soon. The perceptive mentor will welcome this enthusiasm but not confuse it with competence and may anticipate some setbacks before long. Conversely, some students will remain very distant and unsure of themselves and will need help in building up their confidence. In both cases, the mentor will be providing support, albeit at different stages.

The mentor can support the student in a variety of ways. In the first instance she will be acting as a mediator between students and other members of the department, helping to negotiate which classes will be observed and later which ones will be taught. This may require some diplomacy on her part. At a practical level she will make sure that students have access to resources and to essentials like stockroom keys and paper for photocopiers. Sometimes she, and other members of the department will be acting as a friend to students, getting to know them, and sharing their worries and their successes. When things go wrong she may simply be there to listen and empathise, and even to help students see the funny side of the situation.

For real learning, however, it is the effective combination of support and challenge described by Daloz (1986) which is necessary. Having a mentor who is a good teacher can be a challenge in itself, but robust feedback after lessons which probes the students' thinking, questions their actions and pushes them onwards is also needed. As an important assessor, the mentor needs to share ongoing judgements and be open about weaknesses which need to be overcome and progress which needs to be made. This is difficult to do – nobody likes being confronted with their weaknesses and few people relish the prospect of being the confronter! It is easier to criticise people behind their backs to other members of staff, or the IHE tutor, but professional mentors should not resort to this.

As school-based training has become widespread, challenge and support and the relationship between them have come under closer scrutiny from researchers. In a range of studies (e.g. Abell *et al.*, 1995) the almost consistent picture which is emerging is one in which the support role dominates the challenge role. For instance, in a study of primary mentors and beginning teachers (Cameron-Jones and O'Hara, 1997), the degree of challenge which teachers perceived they were offering was not felt as strongly by the students. The researchers' conclusion was that challenge may have been given to students but that '. . . support by its nature might "kill" the intent, expression or impact of challenge when the two are present in combination.'

Clearly this research needs to be taken on board by mentors and IHE tutors when they meet to discuss issues in the partnership, but it seems to me that students need to be party to these insights as well. They need to be aware that mentors may be offering advice and encouragement, but in the student's need for affirmation the advice may not be heard. This is where written feedback is invaluable. Informal conversations are important, but they are easily forgotten and people's words and intentions may be misinterpreted.

As time goes on, students should become more proactive in their own learning, although many remain very dependent on their mentors and tutors. One way of becoming more involved is to prepare intentionally for discussions with the mentor. When the student is observing, this may simply be:

- Asking *why* the mentor/teacher made certain decisions in the classroom.
- Asking the mentor/teacher *how* she actually prepared that lesson.
- Asking the mentor/teacher if she is satisfied with the lesson and *what* she would change in the future.

When the mentor is observing the student may:

- Ask the mentor to make non-evaluative notes which they can discuss together afterwards.
- Ask the mentor to focus on one particular aspect of the lesson, or a small group of pupils.

But this is probably going too far too fast for this chapter. Students need to get off to a good start in their important relationship with their mathematics mentor and they need to:

- remember that students are placed in schools to learn, and that in the early stages of training they should not be expected to be competent;

- be sensitive to the rules and routines in school, e.g. punctuality;
- use time set aside for discussions with the mentor sensibly, e.g. have a list of questions;
- give the mentor some space to get on with her other responsibilities;
- be open about concerns;
- enjoy friendship and support but not at the expense of recognising challenging opportunities which the mentor can offer;
- remember that the mentor can be torn between holding and letting go (Watson, 1994);
- remember that other people, e.g. fellow students, newly qualified teachers, can also offer support and advice.

Finally, the mentor-student relationship is affected by the differing personalities and values of the people involved. Some students and mentors remain friends long after the practice, and some are glad to say goodbye to each other. Teachers do not have to like all their pupils to treat them with respect and give them good learning opportunities – the same is true for students and their mentors.

REFERENCES

Abell, S.K., Dillon, D.R., Hopkins, C.J., McInerny, W.D. and O'Brien, D.G. (1995) 'Somebody to count on: mentor/intern relationships in a beginning teacher internship program', *Teaching and Teacher Education*, **11**, 173–88.

Brown, C.A. (1992) 'Becoming a mathematics teacher', in *Handbook on Research on Mathematics Teaching and Learning*, D.A. Grouws (ed.). New York: Macmillan.

Cameron-Jones, M. and O'Hara, P. (1997) 'Support and challenge in teacher education', *British Educational Research Journal*, **23**(1), 15–23.

Daloz, L. (1986) *Effective Teaching and Mentoring*. San-Francisco: Jossey-Bass.

Gates, P. (1994) 'A focus on learning to teach', in *Mentoring in Mathematics Teaching*, B. Jaworski and A. Watson (eds). Lewes: Falmer.

Haggerty, L. (1995) *New Ideas for Teacher Education*. London: Cassell.

Lacey, C. (1977) *The Socialization of Teachers*. London: Methuen.

Watson, A. (1994) 'A mentor's eye view', in *Mentoring in Mathematics Teaching*, B. Jaworski and A. Watson (eds). Lewes: Falmer.

5: Making sense of observations

OBSERVATION ACTIVITIES

As observations on the serial visits begin, the dual role of outsider and insider may be very demanding for the student teacher. On the one hand, as an observer it is very tempting to focus upon the class teacher exclusively and to analyse his or her classroom behaviour in a very critical way. On the other, it may be tempting to assume that there is no room for manoeuvre – that the student will need to reproduce the class teacher's routines and approaches since these are tried and tested and any deviation will result in disaster. As time goes on, this focus on the teacher may be relaxed and greater attention may be paid to the pupils and their learning.

Most courses adopt a pattern of observation with a gradual build-up into teaching full classes, and structure is built into this by the provision of observation schedules of various forms. At the very lowest level these may be seen as something with which to keep students busy before they are launched into teaching classes. Although this is clearly not a good reason in itself, there is something to be said for having a focus when acting as an observer and for getting to know the pupils in a class and how their regular teacher works with them at the same time. In short, the student may feel less of a spare part. If the focus of the observation is one which will give her an important insight into certain organisational features, or teaching strategies, or ways in which the teacher ensures maximum class involvement, then this is clearly useful and may help her in future planning decisions. Paradoxically, the process of structured lesson observation may be most useful when the student has done some teaching already and recognises the significance of certain classroom decisions, which may be lost on novice teachers.

To illustrate this point, consider these two sequences of teacher talk:

'What is the value of cos $0°$? What is the value of cos $90°$? What happens to the value of cos as the angle increases from $0°$ to $90°$?'

'Each person write down three angles bigger than $0°$ and smaller than $90°$ and find the value of their cosines using a calculator.

Amy, can you tell me the smallest value for cosine out of your three angles? Which angle was that for?

Sam, what was the largest value you had? Which angle was that the cosine of? Has anyone got a smaller value than Amy's smallest?'

(Teacher takes several responses and writes them on the board.)

'Has anyone got smaller than this (pointing to a value)? What's the smallest cosine we can get? What angle is it for? How about the biggest we can get? What angle is it for? Do you notice anything here?'

Although the mathematical content of both sequences is very similar, there is a subtle difference between the teacher talk in each. In the first there is a very compressed set of questions, unambiguous and concise. The first two are closed and the third admits of little variation of response. In the second sequence, the questions are far more wordy, the teacher has deliberately invited a range of responses so that everyone is a potential contributor, and the unfamiliar idea of the cosine as a *decreasing* function for angles between 0° and 90° is being gradually built up. The teacher is also making an implicit distinction between the angle and its cosine by asking specific questions and by the use of different sides of the board for recording.

An inexperienced student may not see the importance of the differences here, until she has experienced the difficulties which many pupils have with apparently straightforward mathematical ideas. She may not realise the way in which closed questions can shut off an activity for pupils almost before it has begun, but how specific questions like the one to Amy may be productive in giving a starting point for the later questions. She may also miss the importance of context – that the first set of questions may be appropriate for a class consolidating or revising the topic, whilst the second set may be more appropriate in the early stages of a topic or when the teacher is keen to assess the class's emergent understanding before moving on too quickly. By writing down examples of such oral exchanges, as an observation activity, and then bringing them back for discussion in tutorials, the student may be sensitised to such differences and begin to gain a richer understanding of the possibilities of classroom talk.

It seems to me that although the ability to use observation periods fruitfully will vary between students, there is room for a developmental approach throughout the year. There is a very good case for observing when teaching practice is well established, when a student finds herself in difficulties and needs to backtrack, or when a particular feature of classroom interaction is of special interest to the student. Moreover, the pro forma which are issued for observation activities are sometimes difficult to use and do not seem to fit the situation being observed. As the practice progresses it may be more fruitful for students to identify issues of importance to them, and to decide how they will record observation data for themselves.

THE SENSITIVITIES OF OBSERVATIONS

In many schools, teachers are used to having other people with them in their lessons. For instance, support teachers may be there to help particular pupils with learning difficulties, or in primary schools it is relatively common to find parents helping with reading or with computing. None the less, having an observer can be an uncomfortable experience when the two people are still getting to know each other. For students, the first introduction is very important to them and it is only good practice for the teacher to introduce the student in a professional way:

> 'This is Miss Gibbon. She'll be watching the lesson today and in a few weeks she'll be teaching you. Once you have started you can ask her for help as well as me.'

Some are sensitive about being called students but others do not mind this as long as the introduction is done clearly and respectfully. Since this matters so much, it is worth asking the teacher how he will make this introduction before the lesson starts. Between the teacher and the student, a suitable form of words should then be agreed and an unfortunate beginning can be avoided. Before the lesson, the focus of the observation should also be agreed. The teacher will feel less sensitive if he knows what is being written down, and if he has any objections to parts of the schedule he can let these be known. Anything written down should also be shared with the teacher as soon as possible after the lesson. This is only good manners but it is also an opportunity for the beginning of a reflective dialogue with the teacher.

It is a good idea to try to empathise with the teacher. Before my students go into school, I ask them to do an exercise to heighten their awareness of this issue. They have to think of themselves in two roles, as an observer and as a teacher being observed, and they fill in possible endings to the following statements:

1. *Observer*:
   I want the teacher I am observing to . . .
   I do not want the teacher I am observing to . . .
2. *Being observed*:
   I want the observer to . . .
   I do not want the observer to . . .

Examples of responses have been:

- I want the teacher I am observing to:
  – be in control
  – teach in an interesting way
  - be confident . . . .
- I do not want the teacher I am observing to:
  – be too perfect
  – be too harsh with the pupils.
- I want the observer to:
  – be unobtrusive
  – get involved with the pupils.
- I do not want the observer to:
  – write things down and not show me
  – be too critical.

An exercise like this not only helps students to see things from the teacher's perspective, but it encourages them to think about how they will behave as observers. For instance, there is nothing more irritating for a teacher to see a student sitting immobile at the back of the class doing nothing when they could be walking around, getting to know pupils' names and finding out how they are thinking about the mathematics. If, however, the student has negotiated a particular focus for lesson observation then the teacher will understand why she is not participating and there will be understanding on both sides.

HOW STUDENTS USE STRUCTURED OBSERVATIONS

Collecting data for the sake of it soon becomes boring. Unless the information feeds into tutorials in the IHE, or is shared with the class teacher as a way of getting him to articulate his practice, or is summarised and used for reflection by the student teacher there is little point. When mathematics students are placed in pairs, comparing observations on different classes may be fruitful, as can observations from students of other subjects.

In 'The shape of a lesson' observation activity (Example 5.1), one student managed to pack a great deal of detail into his notes, and then was able to see a very similar lesson with a different group. It was very interesting to me that these notes did not fit the preconceived format of the observation schedule, and that the student's attention was fixed much more on the content of the lesson. When this was brought back to the HE tutorial, however, the detail made for a very rich discussion. In particular, the very open starting activity provoked a variety of responses. Some thought it was a good way to get pupils involved, and some thought it was deceptive, since the teacher knew which definition of square numbers he really wanted to come out of the activity. We also debated the transition and how it could have been handled differently. For the pupils who had simply arranged counters to form the digits

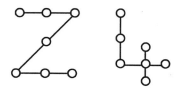

it was felt that the pupils needed to realise that any number could be constructed in that way, and so calling it a square number would have no special significance. It was also felt that there was a great deal to be gained from exploring the 'hollow' square numbers as well as the 'full' ones, since these both had interesting properties and had arisen from the pupils' work. The students' comments about the second lesson were squeezed out but the issue of attainment and ability was revisited over and over in subsequent tutorials, with my own contribution invariably warning against having low expectations and creating self-fulfilling prophesies.

A contrasting use of the same observation sheet is given in Example 5.2. Here the student has used it more or less in the manner intended and we do not have the same feel for the content of the lesson. The general shape is of a lesson sandwiched between two separate activities – a tables test, and a concluding quiz. Although there are some implied criticisms, the student also recognises the effectiveness of the routines in maintaining the pace and flow of the lesson. When discussing observations of this type, students were able to share introductory and concluding activities which they had seen in schools, and were thus alerted to simple techniques which can be effective but are easily overlooked. This aspect of their work has improved considerably since the discussion of this observation schedule.

In the final example of an observation schedule (Example 5.3), the focus this time is on classroom interactions. Here the student and others who managed to complete this observation, felt that several factors determined the interactions in the classroom and that sex differences were not particularly noticeable. Ability and confidence were cited as factors determining how often teachers and pupils would interact in a lesson, and these factors were seen as being independent of gender. Many of them were alerted to pupils who had no interactions with the teacher at all during the lesson, and one of the students remarked that the sheet had been useful in raising her own awareness of how unacknowledged prejudices could influence the quantity and quality of her own exchanges in the future.

In fact there are some differences between boys and girls in the data, girls being nominated to answer questions more, with boys tending to answer without being nominated and there are also differences between the use of praise and reprimands. I am very sensitive to these differences and perhaps have a more researcherly eye for potentially significant classroom patterns. For me, these differences point to an interesting line for further enquiry in this classroom, but student teachers are coming to this with less experience, a different perspective and with a different purpose. At this stage, the observation activities may simply alert students to aspects of classroom life which could remain hidden. They offer students the opportunity to notice and mentally mark particular events. Sustained and systematic enquiry may have to wait awhile.

Example 5.1 The shape of a lesson

Lessons often take place within a framework which may consist of taken-for-granted rules and routines. There may be several phases to the lesson, and teachers may indicate transitions by particular instructions, tone of voice or non-verbal communication. Pupils may also indicate their own informal rules in a variety of ways.

This observation activity is intended to give you an opportunity to look at this aspect of the classroom in more depth. For instance, how do teachers attract the attention of the pupils in order to state a rule, give some help to the whole class or in order to make a transition? You may wish to make a note of the words or gestures used to attract attention. You may then wish to make a note of the words and phrases used when the teacher has gained attention and is moving into the next phase of activity. You will also learn a great deal by writing down pupils' words and phrases which indicate their response to the pace and flow of the lesson determined by the teacher.

Observe a lesson to familiarise yourself with this observation framework and then make brief notes on a later lesson.

Class 7, top set, very capable, quick on the uptake

1. Entry phase:
   - Talk
   - Movement
   - Time
   - Teacher–pupil communication
   - Pupil–pupil communication

   10.05 'We are going to talk about "square numbers". We have never talked about them before. Why do you think they might be? Use coloured counters to make what you think might be a square number. Whatever you think they should be. Use your imagination. Nobody will be wrong because I haven't told you anything. Just think of a few ideas.' [Teacher from front of the class] Some kids look puzzled and look at teacher, me, each other for inspiration.

2. Settling-down phase:
   - Talk
   - Movement
   - Time
   - Teacher–pupil communication
   - Pupil–pupil communication

   10.10 Lots of discussion between pupils, and most soon started experimenting with counters. Several times kids asked 'if this is all right', to be met with typical response, 'If you think it is.' [Teacher/me walking about] Some kids formed numbers in a square shape, others formed numbers symbols with the counters, some made piles of counters, others made empty squares, some filled them in. All made an attempt at doing something and those who made the number 4 and actual squares seemed to have a good idea of what it was all about.

3. Lesson proper:
   - Talk
   - Movement
   - Time
   - Teacher-pupil communication
   - Teacher-pupil communication

10.20   [Teacher at front of the class] 'In maths, square numbers mean to arrange counters in a square.' 'How do we know it is a square?' 'Because each side is the same. Make a square with 4 counters . . . now try 6. Silly question really. What might the next square number be?' '9' 'Why' 'Because each side is 3 counters long.' Kids soon caught on with 16(4 × 4), 25(5 × 5) . . . . 'Is 1 a square number?' 'Counters away. In exercise books, draw first 5 square numbers. Quickly, you've got 5 mins.' [On board] 'Against each square write 1 × 1, 2 × 2, 3 × 3 . . . What does this mean [1²]? One squared or 1 raised to the power of 2. Always write power numbers smaller than the main number.' 'What might 2 × 2 be written as?' Children asked for 3 × 3, 4 × 4 etc., until they all got the idea. Then recap. 'So 6 × 6 = 6² = 36 . . . digit sum 9.' 'Do tables for first 20 numbers, write multiples and digit sums.' [Walking around noted that 7 × 7 = 49 DS 13. On board, I told them this became DS 4.] 'Look at DS's What are the numbers? [on board] 1, 4, 9, 7, 7, 9 . . . Can you see a pattern? Not like other patterns, but it does repeat, doesn't it?'

4. Clearing-up phase:
   - Talk
   - Movement
   - Time
   - Teacher–pupil communication
   - Pupil–pupil communication

10.50   Paper issued to draw 3D shapes. Children shown how to draw a unit cube, then 2 unit cube. Some kids find it very difficult to draw 2 unit cube even though 1 unit cube is drawn OK. 'Split 2 unit cubes up into 1 unit cubes. How many 1 unit cubes fits inside the 2 unit cubes? Now draw 3 and 4 unit cubes.' [Multilink then used to show how cube sizes build up and also how many single cubes make up the larger cubes.] '1 unit cube is 1 × 1 × 1, anyone know a quick way to write that?' '1³' 'Same goes for 2 × 2 × 2 = 2³.'

5. Exit phase:
   - Talk
   - Movement
   - Time
   - Teacher-pupil communication
   - Pupil-pupil communication

11.05   Counters away, pencils down, listen to me. For homework tonight, draw on triangular dot paper 3D diagrams of 1 unit cube, 2 unit, 3 and 4 unit cubes. Write down how many small unit cubes make each bigger unit cube.

Reflection

The lesson with 7Y1 went very well, with no need to particularly halt the flow at any stage. The children, virtually without exception, appeared to grasp the concept of square numbers very quickly. Fortuitously, the same lesson was planned for an older, but somewhat 'less able' class, later in the day. This proved to be far more revealing.

Class 8Y3
Lesson started in the same way, same introduction, same sort of queries. Similar counter experiences resulted, one child formed the number 36 with counters and told me it was 6 x 6, but his friend had copied the same idea to make 24.

Same process followed $2 \times 2 = 4$, $3 \times 3 = 9$, $4 \times 4 = 16$ 'What is next in the sequence?' 'Why are they called square numbers?' 'Because they can be arranged in a square.'

It was noticeable throughout the lesson, how class responded less and teacher had to guide them more. I had noticed this with other ability groups to the extent, that, when bottom groups 6/6 were taught, it was a case of teacher having to do significantly more talking, especially by way of explanation to kids and not expecting a great deal of response to questions.

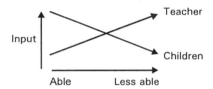

Squares drawn in books, the number and digit sums from 1^2 to 20^2. Patterns identified. Then change of tack followed:

'How would we work out 2^2+3^2? What is 2^2?'
'4'

'What is 3^2?'
'9'

'So the answer to 2^2+3^2 is?'
'13'

'Let's do $6^2 - 5^2 = 36 - 25 = 11$
                  $5^2 - 4^2 = 25 - 16 = 9$
                  $4^2 - 3^2 = 16 - 9 = 7$

'Can you see a pattern? Gets 2 smaller.'

'How could I have got an answer of 13?'
'$7^2 - 6^2$'

'What happens if we add them?

Example 5.2   The shape of a lesson

1. Entry phase:
   - Talk   *'OK, to the back of your books. Routine × tables'*
   - Movement
   - Time   *about 10 mins*
   - Teacher–pupil communication   *Q/A session else teacher dictating but they*
                                                       ***did** recite × table first*
   - Pupil–pupil communication   *minimal – only in marking each other's work*
2. Settling-down phase:
   - Talk   *'What were we doing last time?'*
   - Movement   *at blackboard*
   - Time   *about 10 mins*
   - Teacher–pupil communication   *Q/A, no Q from pupils, positive responses from T*
   - Pupil–pupil communication   *no*
3. Lesson proper:
   - Talk   *'Rule off, write heading . . . go'*
   - Movement   *T moves around to individuals, children ask*
                                                       Qs now
   - Time   *10 mins*
   - Teacher–pupil communication   *one to one*
   - Pupil–pupil communication   *very little*
4. Clearing-up phase:
   - Talk   *'OK, leave your work'*
   - Movement   *waits . . . back to board*
   - Time   *5 mins*
   - Teacher–pupil communication   *what we've learnt Q/A, homework*
   - Pupil–pupil communication   *none*
5. Exit phase:
   - Talk   *quiz – not related to lesson*
   - Movement   *fidgety, but **do** wait and try to answer*
   - Time   *5 mins*
   - Teacher–pupil communication   *fun – relaxed – not strict about answers*
   - Pupil–pupil communication   *quietly puzzling answers*

Reflection

Examples of rules and routines. How were they conveyed? Was this effective?
'rule off' 'put books down' 'x tables first'
pupils were used to it, effective

Teacher's decisions. Can you identify reasons behind the teacher's decisions?
To recap, to move on, to summarise
Qs asked often by kids in circulating

Write down instances where the pupils were indicating a transition in the lesson. Did the teacher respond?
No, he was in full stride! Bored after 10+ mins of blackboard work, overly recapping no sequences. Fidget, Arms stop going up – look in bags etc.

Example 5.3 Classroom interaction

Structured observation schedules like the one below have their limitations. Sometimes it is hard to categorise events. None the less, try this one with different teachers and with different classroom layouts and see if there are any patterns. Your first one may be quite difficult to do so try more than once and make your own modifications to the code, plan etc.

Mark these interactions on a seating plan. Indicate where the boys and girls are sitting and then use this code during the lesson (use a tally next to the letter).

Teacher nominates pupil: N
Pupil answers question: P
Pupil asks question: A
Teacher works with individual: I
Teacher reprimands pupil: R
Teachers praises pupil: Pr
Pupil disrupts others: D
Teacher shares joke with pupil: J

Girl: **G**
Boy: **B**

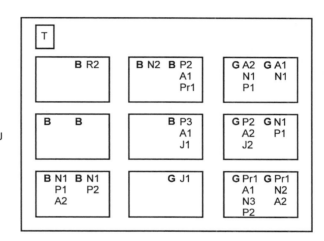

Summarise:

	Tally – Girls	Total	Tally – Boys	Total
Teacher nominates pupil: N	ЖНΙ IIII	9	ЖНΙ	4
Pupil answers question: P	ЖНΙ I	6	ЖНΙ III	8
Pupil asks question: A	ЖНΙ I	6	IIII	4
Teacher works with individual : I				
Teacher reprimands pupil: R			II	2
Teacher praises pupil: Pr	II	2	I	1
Pupil disrupts others: D				
Teacher shares joke: J	III	3	I	1

6: Lessons for learning

I have observed many mathematics lessons in schools, both before and after the introduction of school-based courses. I also have videotapes of lessons which student teachers have taught, and it is in watching these that I have been struck by the levels of interpretation which are afforded by rewatching the same lesson. This, of course, is not possible in real time. The teacher is constantly thinking in action during the lesson, and the observer, freed from the responsibility of teaching, has a similarly complex role. The aspects of the lesson picked out as significant by the observer may depend upon what has been mutually agreed; they may be heavily influenced by the observer's values and priorities, and whether all these aspects are discussed at the end of the lesson may depend on judgements about the stage of the student's development, the student's confidence, and readiness to engage with particular issues. Besides, the student may well have selected different aspects as critical.

It is much easier to think about these issues in the context of real lessons taught by real student teachers – the approach adopted in this chapter. The reader, however, will need to be aware that interpretations are being offered, albeit based on field notes, and that this in itself is a step away from reality. The lessons themselves have been chosen because they illustrate aspects of children's learning in the classroom situation, they present opportunities for speculation about alternative strategies or future plans, and they were all lessons in which both the students and I were happy with events. Indeed, by my values, I judged some of the lessons to be very good. The lessons were all taught in state comprehensive schools, most without large percentages of pupils attaining high grades in public examinations, with a range of topics, year groups and settings. Interspersed through the text are suggestions which the reader may like to work on or discuss with peers.

THE QUADRILATERALS LESSON

The context

Mary was a student teacher with a few years unqualified teaching experience before she did her PGCE. Before this lesson, she warned me that she had found this middle set of Year 9 (13–14 year olds) pupils quite difficult to control and that her own expectations of behaviour and work rate contrasted with the usual class teacher's. She wanted a more purposeful atmosphere in the class, and this was beginning to happen after a few weeks of the first teaching practice. As I arrived, Mary was already in the classroom with two pupils who had taken charge of setting out felt-tip pens and dotty paper, rather than face the inclement weather in the school yard. The room itself was large with tables arranged in a U shape and an OHP with screen at the front.

Having tried a structured investigation with the class earlier in the week, Mary was taking a risk and trying a completely open-ended activity. The idea came from a worksheet, but Mary wanted to abandon this and organise the activity herself. Essentially, the idea was for pupils to draw quadrilaterals on the spotty paper and then classify them according to their own rules. The only restriction was that the quadrilaterals had to fit within a nine dot square.

Readers may like to do this investigation themselves at this point.

The lesson

At the beginning of the lesson, Mary held up two displays of the pupils' previous work on tessellations which were attractively presented. This immediately caught the pupils' attention and they were clearly pleased with the result, pointing out their contributions to each other. This meant that Mary already had a captive audience and introduced the task using an OHP. She started with the nine dot square and invited pupils to say how a four-sided shape could be drawn. The first one volunteered was the large square:

and then another pupil asked if you could go smaller than the nine pin square:

On a second acetate she had labelled the points with numbers so the pupils could now identify more shapes by saying how to join the numbered points. A variety of shapes were volunteered and the pupils were asked if they could remember 'the posh mathematical name for four sided shapes'. Someone could.

At this point, Mary asked the pupils to continue this themselves on their spotty paper, and when they had drawn quite a few to group them together. The way she phrased this was to say 'Look at your shapes, and decide which ones go together for some reason'. She stressed that there were no right answers, and that everyone would end up with a different result.

The pupils had been completely attentive up to now and made the transition to individual work with little fuss. As Mary went round she kept on reminding tentative pupils that there were only two rules – the shapes had to be a quadrilateral and they had to fit inside the nine pin square. The way in which the pupils drew and classified their shapes was up to them.

This activity now took up the bulk of the lesson and the pupils remained engaged in their work. Many of them started with squares and rectangles, but soon started to branch out, producing a variety of four-sided shapes:

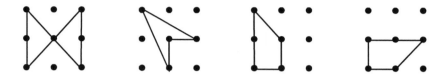

Shapes like the last two caused some discussion between pupils and Mary as she circulated around the class, and this fed into their later classifications. One girl said she was going to put shapes with the same area together, and when probed she said she meant shapes which could be turned around to fit on top of each other. This moved the attention away from area in its conventional sense and more towards the idea of translating shapes through rotation, but she may have been indicating her understanding that area remained invariant under rotation.

Another boy had begun his classification and had grouped these three shapes together:

He explained that the first shape was a square, the second was a square if it was turned around, and the third could be stretched to make a square. He showed me what he meant visually with his thumb and forefinger doing an imaginary stretch on his diagram, pulling the top-right corner to the right and the bottom-left corner to the left. I did not comment, but with hindsight I wonder if some more probing would have been a good idea. Was there something special about this particular kind of stretch, which linked the squares together?

Readers may like to speculate about possible interventions at this point.

Pupils handled the recording of the grouping in different ways. Some decided to colour code the shapes on the original sheets and then explain their reasoning on another sheet of paper. Some did the grouping on another sheet and re-drew their shapes according to the classification. Again it was their decision. As the end of the lesson drew nearer, Mary wanted to make sure that everyone had started on this stage. Most had, but there were one or two still drawing shapes. This may have been for a variety of reasons – they may have wanted to draw every possible shape and had not yet finished, or they were avoiding the classification because they were unsure about it. This is always a tricky classroom decision, because the first of the two reasons is very sensible in the context of the task and the second is an understandable strategy if the pupil does not feel ready to take a risk.

At the end of the lesson, Mary asked them about their groupings. She wrote up ideas on the OHP as pupils volunteered them. Again she had a few tricky decisions and in some cases she adapted the exact words which the children used. Some contributions were:

- Basic shapes
- The number of dots the shape covers – how many dots on the outside and how many on the inside.

  (*Readers may like to investigate this themselves. What are the possibilities? Can you get eight dots?*)

- Rotations (adapted from 'shapes which when you turn them round look different').
- Extraordinary shapes.
- Shapes with right angles.
- Pointiness (adapted from 'some shapes are basic shapes but other go in and out').

At this point the lesson had come to an end and the pupils helped to collect in the work and equipment, and made their way out peacefully. There was no stampede for the door, and one pupil was heard to remark that he had enjoyed the lesson – 'it was a nice change'.

Afterwards

Mary was very pleased with the way the lesson had gone, although she felt that the excellent working atmosphere had been helped by the absence of a few pupils. Also, it was a 'first' for her since she had never tried anything like it before. She had intended to press on more quickly but realised during the lesson that the pupils needed plenty of time to get into the task and she did not want to spoil this. She was, however, in a dilemma about how to follow on. Her principal aim had been to see how the pupils responded to an open-ended task, and she had originally been less concerned about the quadrilaterals and their classification. The activity, however, highlighted the very diverse ways in which the pupils saw their quadrilaterals, and the very different use of mathematical properties and associated language which had arisen around the class. Mary was dubious about following on with an imposed classification because she had told the pupils that there were no right answers. On the other hand, we (the class teacher, Mary and I) all felt that there was more to be had from the activity. One suggestion was for the pupils to read each others' classification, and say if they felt it was clear and convincing. Another was to use the shapes generated and steer the pupils towards more refined mathematical language. Another was to suggest a classification and then ask the pupils to use it to group the class's results. These suggestions were left open for Mary to work on in the spirit of the original lesson but we all agreed that the decision would depend greatly upon what was found from a close reading of the pupils' recording.

THE MYSTIC ROSE LESSON

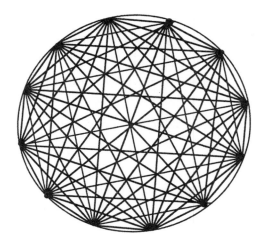

The context

Sean was working with a mixed-ability Year 7 (age 11–12) class of 25 pupils, ranging from one extremely bright pupil and a few who were given in-class support from a special needs teacher. They had been working with enjoyment on curve stitching pictures, but Sean had been surprised at the low level of accurate construction skills in the class. Since there was limited access to computer aided design for these pupils he felt this was a legitimate learning objective.

The lesson

Sean wanted the pupils to be able to see how a mystic rose could be constructed and then to practise their construction skills (lines and angles) by creating their own. He shared this aim with the pupils at the beginning of the lesson. Initially, they looked at a mystic rose in their text books and he asked them 'How would you draw this?'

Readers may like to think about this themselves before reading on.

There were several suggestions about drawing the initial circle and marking points around the circumference. It was clear that some pupils were trying to measure the distance between the circumference points in the textbook but were unable to extend this to working with the much larger circle which Sean had now drawn on the board. At this point, he made the instant decision to give a hint about looking at the angles at the centre of the circle.

Could he have stayed with the idea of equally spaced points around the circumference? What might have happened?

The high-attaining boy immediately responded to the hint

> 'You divide the number of points around the outside into 360 degrees'

and Sean then explored this suggestion by going for particular values – 4, 5 and then 18 points on the circumference. Most, but not all, of the pupils claimed to understand this and were responding to questions. Some admitted they did not understand and Sean promised to go through it again with them individually. It was noticeable, however, that they had not switched off and were able to accept this calculation for the time being. Pupils talked Sean through the use of the protractor – he was marking off every 20 degrees – and this refreshed recent work they had been doing about angles. Once the points were marked pupils were asked how to carry on:

> 'Sir, the lines all sprag out from the bottom.'
> 'Every point is joined to every other point.'

Sean demonstrated for one of the points and said 'We're getting a nice pattern already' to which one pupils responded 'It's like a shell'.

It was now time for the constructions to begin, using a pre-prepared worksheet. Previous marked work was handed out, which indicated which of three versions of the rose should be attempted. This was where differentiation was in operation. One version repeated the instructions and explanations for the 18-point rose, the second gave a centre angle of 15 degrees and in the last version pupils had to work out their own angle for a 20-point rose and then construct it. Pupils made the transition quickly and were soon down to work. Some had a previous pattern to finish but Sean discouraged unnecessary colouring in and encouraged pupils to move on. Equipment was given out by pupils, Sean saw the pupils who had not understood the angle calculation and the support teacher was able to go through this with her pupils. Having the angle indicators in front of them made this much easier.

Right at the end of the lesson, the first rose had been completed, but most pupils were well on the way and were told they would be able to complete them next lesson.

What would you do next lesson as pupils finished at different points? Think of connected extension activities or challenges which could be set for these pupils. Avoid giving them more of the same.

Afterwards

Sean was satisfied with the lesson, and I felt that he had done very well in encouraging the pupils' language and in giving them an accessible task which was both satisfying and visually pleasing. The support teacher was very happy – she had been able to give her pupils the extra help they needed but had felt that they were well catered for in the lesson. We talked about possible extension activities but also about how the work would be assessed and feedback given. The possibility of negotiating assessment criteria with the pupils was also discussed.

FRACTIONS AND DECIMALS

The context

Katya and Simone were working in a pair with a mixed-ability Year 7 class. In this school the lower attainers were taken out of the mathematics lesson and taught separately, but there was still a wide range of attainment and understanding. This was particularly discernible in the topic under question, and the two students had decided to maximise their pairing by working in a team with the class. This seemed to be a very intelligent response to an opportunity offered on teaching practice, which they may not have again in the near future. They had used a variety of conventional teaching approaches to the topic, but were still not satisfied by the pupils' progress and had been greatly exercised by trying to differentiate their tasks for the class.

The lesson

As a change, but also to give all the pupils some sense of success at the end of the topic, the two students had split the class into two mixed attainment groups to work on two fractions and decimals games:

- Game 1 – Fractions and decimals dominoes.
- Game 2 – Fractions and decimals pairs.

For the first game, Simone had created several very large dominoes out of card and demonstrated the way they could be put together. She had chosen a variety of representations, e.g.

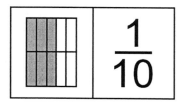   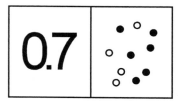

Readers may like to think of other possibilities.

Pupils said how they could be put together and there was clearly some confusion still about certain equivalences, e.g. equivalences for the left side of the first domino in which 3/5 is shaded. Simone explained this to them using equivalent fractions.

For the second game, a small pack of cards had already been created. On each there was a single representation of a decimal or fraction. Pupils were to be dealt a small number of cards and then take it in turns to turn over the top card from the pack. The player then had to suggest or draw an equivalent representation. If anyone had that card or another equivalence they could claim a pair. The player with the most pairs at the end of the game would be the winner.

Once both games had been explained, the pairs group had a game with the existing cards. When this was finished they were to work together to create a new pack of cards. The dominoes group were given a sheet with 16 outline dominoes drawn in. They were to create their own set of dominoes making sure that the second representation on the first domino matched the first on the next etc. Once they had a set they could cut them out and play with their partner.

Simone's involvement in the domino game was less necessary now that the pupils had started. She helped them if they were stuck, or checked their representations and encouraged pupils to try harder examples. Katya, on the other hand, was much more directly involved since there was quite a bit of discussion in this group of about ten pupils. It took quite a long time to play out the game and there was limited time for the pupils to start making their own pairs. None the less they were very absorbed throughout the lesson, as were the dominoes group.

By the end of the lesson several dominoes games had been played in the pairs and a new set of pairs cards was in the process of being made. There was a brief conclusion when some previous marked work was handed out and a puzzle challenge was set for homework.

Afterwards

Simone and Katya remarked that they knew I would enjoy the lesson and they were right. These were my written comments on the feedback sheets at the end of the lesson:

> 'This was a lovely lesson. It was nice to have the pair of you and the class teacher but I think either of you could manage this by yourself in the future. Either activity could be done with a mixed-ability class because they can both be differentiated according to the level of the pupils' understanding. The idea was particularly good for diagnostic assessment – getting the pupils to explain to each other and to the teacher gives you a good idea of their understandings. You could also use the idea in other topics – percentages, number operations, algebra ($(a + b)^2 = a^2 + b^2 + 2ab$, $ab = ba$, $a^2b = a*a*b$ . . .) The social spin-offs were also very worthwhile; pupils were working in pairs on a cooperative activity. Most of them were having a very good time and reinforcing important understandings. This lesson was a tonic!'

FAIR GAMES

The context

Unfortunately the lesson I am about to describe happened a long time ago and I no longer have my lesson notes, so I am describing it from memory. It has stuck in my mind as one of those rare mathematics lessons in which pupils considered people's everyday behaviour in the context of a mathematical concept. Alan was on his first practice with a small special needs class of Year 9 pupils, and a support teacher was in the lesson helping individuals. A great deal of trouble had gone into making the spinners for one of the two probability games which were played. These were made of triangles of cardboard with a sharpened matchstick spinner:

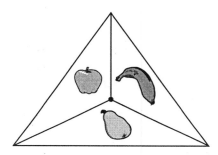

The pupils were paired, given twenty counters each, and asked to nominate themselves as player 1 or player 2. They were to spin the spinner twice – if it landed on the same fruit twice player 1 took a counter, otherwise player 2 took a counter. The winner was the one with the most counters at the end. When several games had been played, class results were pooled. It turned out that for all the pairs, player 2 had won each time. Pupils were invited to say why, and in the class discussion which followed all the possible winning combinations were drawn out. Pupils were able to see why a banana on the first spin and an apple on the second was different from an apple on the first and a banana on the second, even though they would both be winning spins for player 2.

The second game was weighted more finely. From memory, this was a two dice game. Player 1 would win if the total on the two dice was greater than or equal to 7, player 2 if the total was less than or equal to 6. After each pair had at least one game with 20 counters at stake, results were pooled. In the whole class, the player 1s had notched up the greatest number of wins, but there were some wins from the player 2's. Again, the possible outcomes were derived by the class. In neither game was the actual probability of winning calculated, but the general conclusion was that for the second game it was possible to win if you were player 2, but not as easy if you were player 1. Many pupils felt that it was impossible to win on the first game if you were player 1.

If you wanted to compare probabilities for these games with a class, what would you do?

Alan's aim had been for the pupils to see that some games could be rigged so that it was very hard to win. They then went on to talk about slot machines and betting on horses. The pupils were very animated by this discussion and one girl said:

'But people keep on going back to the betting shop even when they don't win . . . '

Would this be an appropriate point for a follow up about people's irrationality, their ignorance of probability, or their inability to resist taking a chance? Are there some cross curricular themes which could be followed up in say English, Religious Education, or Science?

TOPPLING SHAPES

The context

Leyla was approaching the end of her second teaching practice. The school was very happy with her progress and she had by this time been offered a job for the next year. She felt that she had not really had enough experience of pupils working in an investigational or problem-solving mode, and so she had negotiated to work on an investigation with a high-attaining Year 10 class. She told me that she liked the class, but that they were very boisterous and chatty. She also had problems in encouraging everyone to contribute since there were one or two boys who insisted on being first to answer questions and wanted to hold centre stage if they could. The room was very full, with very little room to circulate, and desks were arranged in pairs facing the front.

The lesson

Leyla started by giving some general advice about tackling mathematical problems: trying easy cases, recording results systematically, looking for patterns, trying to generalise either in words or algebraically, trying to predict future outcomes.

Then she introduced the 'Roly Poly investigation' with large shapes at the front of the class.

The idea was to rotate one shape about the other until the original position was achieved with the marked corner in the same place. The first four moves for the triangle about the square are given:

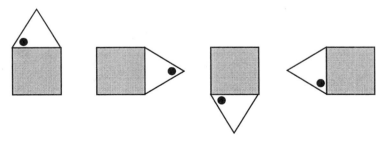

The reader is invited to try continuing the rotations until the triangle returns to its original position at the top of the square with the marked corner at the bottom left.

The pupils in this class were invited to do this with ATM beer mat shapes, starting with the square and triangle as above. A short discussion followed and Leyla moved quickly into the way she wanted the results recorded:

Number of sides of moving shape	Number of sides of still shape	Number of moves	Number of revolutions
3	4	12	3

Pupils then started work on collecting data for different shapes – they could change both the shapes if they wanted. They were soon all busily occupied, and Leyla was able to circulate.

Readers may like to generate their own data at this point.

Pupils were mainly working in pairs, one doing the rotations and the other counting and recording. Patterns started to be generated. Many pupils saw several types of pattern emerging but no overall pattern. For instance, the pupils who had recorded

Number of sides of moving shape	Number of sides of still shape	Number of moves	Number of revolutions
3	4	12	3
4	5	20	4
3	8	24	3
3	6	6	1

felt that their last result was an exception to a rule which seemed to be emerging – that the number in the first and second columns would multiply together to give the third column entry and that the number of revolutions was the same as the number of sides of the revolving shape. Similar exceptions occurred when the two shapes were the square with the octagon, and the square with the hexagon. There was a great deal of genuine excitement and puzzlement in the air, as pupils' predictions were contradicted. The temperature began to rise and the windows steamed up.

It was getting near the end of the lesson so Leyla gathered the class together and collected together results. The general feeling was that there was a pattern but that it did not always work. A general pattern was noticed by one pupil – that the number of sides on the still shape multiplied by the number of revolutions gives the number of moves, but as someone else pointed out this was not much good for prediction since you would need to know the number of revolutions first. Leyla left the puzzle of the pattern for the pupils to think about, as the lesson ended.

Afterwards

Many of Leyla's reservations about the pupils' behaviour had been resolved by the form of the lesson. Liveliness was channelled into work, and enthusiasm had been clearly evident. The dominant boys were not given too many opportunities to show off in front of the whole class and quieter members of the class were fully involved in their smaller groups. The nomination of pupils by name to provide the shared data also gave them a chance to participate fully. It was difficult to assess the mathematical outcomes at this stage as the investigation clearly needed to run further. In particular, the finding of a generally applicable rule and relating this to the geometrical context of the question, rather than just spotting number patterns, was a major aim to be pursued at a later date. Moreover, Leyla had to decide how she would assess the work. The immediate feeling, however, was one of pleasure – pupils reacting well to an unfamiliar experience, and energised by their mathematics.

COMMONALITIES

This selection of lessons certainly reflects some of the values which I, as a mathematics educator, hold. These are demonstrated in views about knowledge, theories of pupils' learning and theories about teaching. We shall return to each of these in later chapters, but an initial exploration is appropriate here.

One common observation is that there was an orderly and purposeful atmosphere in each lesson, and that this was not always the case for these particular classes. There must have been something special in the relationships, choice of activities and organisation which marked these out as successful. Moreover, the topics chosen were all part of the conventional school mathematics curriculum, including the investigational activities.

In Mary's lesson, the pupils' own ways of seeing and thinking were legitimised. She could just as easily have given them definitions of the properties of particular four-sided shapes and asked them to categorise a collection of shapes accordingly. In Alan's lesson, he could have analysed the games theoretically and assessed the fairness by comparing theoretical probabilities. In the paired lesson, pupils could have played dominoes with the teacher's set. There was in all these lessons a shift in emphasis from the teachers' experience and knowledge to that of the pupils. This not only gave them a greater involvement in the process, it gave them an opportunity to generate some knowledge themselves. This is not to say that the teachers did not have an idea of what would happen themselves – Leyla's table was given very early on to guide the investigation in the way she wanted it to go. She could have left things much more open and invited pupils to investigate a range of other avenues – the angles turned by the shapes or the locus traced by the moving vertices – but she probably did not feel confident to handle all these possibilities in the lesson.

By structuring the lessons for pupil involvement, the class as a whole or groups of pupils had greater opportunities to share results and to generate more possibilities. When this happens, it not only increases the range of examples available, but also creates a genuinely social dimension to the learning amongst the pupils themselves. It also increases the demands on the teacher's ability to respond to the unexpected, or to formulate appropriate interventions which will move pupils on. A single characteristic of all the lessons described was the highly interactive nature of the pupil–pupil and teacher–pupil relationship.

Careful thought had gone into the planning of each lesson, and the student teachers explained the tasks clearly. The degree of openness varied – from Mary's quadrilaterals to Sean's mystic roses. Here, Sean's aims had been relatively prosaic but he had set them within a problem-solving situation. The problem – working out how the construction had been done and then drawing the mystic rose – required the pupils to use previous knowledge and skills within a goal-oriented activity. Again, Sean could have reduced this to a set of instructions which pupils merely followed. A small change to this format gave pupils more challenge and the opportunity for differentiation in a mixed-ability class.

In addition, the lessons all provided the teachers with opportunities for formative assessment. The activities provided real insights into the way in which the pupils were seeing and understanding the mathematics, giving all the teachers valuable information which would feed into future teaching decisions.

Finally, there were other aspects of the teaching activities which were very important indicators for future professional development. Many of the lessons represented a calculated risk on behalf of the student teachers. They were breaking with the prevalent teaching style in the department, or trying something they had not done before. In so doing, the students were chancing failure but also giving themselves an opportunity to learn. If student teachers are not prepared to take this risk, they may lose touch with the feelings which accompany learning and may find it more difficult to support pupils upon this road. There was something intangible present in the lessons described – the pupils were motivated, and excited at times, but so were the teachers.

The final lesson to be described is more typical in that some of the previous features described were present and some were not.

THE ORANGE JUICE LESSON

Context

In this lesson the pupils were in Year 10, and the student had not found them to be a particularly easy class to teach. He felt that they were quite lazy and noisy and were not achieving as much as they could. The previous lesson had been devoted to scales – working out real distances given measurements on maps. This lesson was to be about ratios.

The lesson

Large jugs of water, bottles of orange squash and small measuring beakers were available. Philip said he wanted to make 100 ml of orange juice in the ratio of 1:5 and someone immediately said he needed 20 ml of concentrate. The class agreed that this would mean 80 ml of water, but someone soon noticed that this would be in the ratio of 1:4.

'Sir, try 16'

'How much water if it's a ratio of 1:5?'

Several shouted answers – either 84 or 80.

Philip discussed that it would be 80 if the ratio was being used, rather than the total amount and wrote up:

Orange   16
Water   <u>80</u>
           96

and said 'I'm willing to go with that'.

The pupils weren't:

'How about 17?'

'OK, Orange 17, how much water?'

The multiplication by 5 caused several problems but someone eventually offered 85, giving a total of 102 ml.

'Sir, that's better.'

The pupils pushed him again with:

'How about 16.5?'

'Orange 16.5 Water . . . 82.5 . . . total . . . 98.5.'

'Even better.'

'Sir, 16.55.'

'Does anyone know how to do it exactly?'

'Divide by 6.'

The next phase of the activity was for pupils to decide on their own ratio, different from Philip's, to make up the juice to that ratio and then drink it. It was noticeable that many of them chose non-unitary ratios like 2:5 and 3:10, and that many of them had quite sophisticated mental methods for working out the amounts. Others seemed to be copying what their friends were doing and since there was no instruction about working out or recording, they were able to get away with this.

When this was done, the pupils were asked to copy down quite lengthy notes from the board and then follow on with a textbook exercise with questions like:

Divide £42 in the ratio of 2:5.

At this point calculators were brought out and most pupils worked through the exercise in a confident and competent way.

Afterwards

Philip was pleased that the pupils had understood the mathematics and had behaved well during the potentially messy period when they had been making orange juice. He was pleased that they had fallen into his trap at the beginning and gone for the obvious but wrong answer of 20 ml. He was also pleased with the ensuing discussion. He felt that making the orange juice was 'a bit of fun', but that the notes were necessary for exam revision, and the exercise was necessary for consolidation.

My own feeling was that the making of the orange juice was far more than fun and much more could have been made of it. For instance, the pupils could have been asked to record their ratios, and their calculations, even if they had done these in their heads. These could either have been discussed as a whole class, with pupils coming out to explain their work, or the different ratios could have been collected together to form the reinforcement exercise, with the whole class working out each other's calculations. There could also have been some discussion of how the ratio affected the strength of the solution, with some comparisons made where the ratios were not easy to compare directly e.g. 4:7 and 5:8. One or two written examples drawn from the pupils' examples would have been quite sufficient for notes, and all the more memorable for being the pupils' own work.

In this lesson, the pupils were interested, well motivated and well behaved. At the beginning they had been more enthusiastic than the student about pursuing their trial and improvement method and showed a good understanding of zooming in using decimals, although this degree of accuracy would not have been appropriate when measuring out the liquids – a point worth discussing. In this lesson, Philip's risk was in doing practical work with a group he was not sure about, but the pupils rose to the occasion, as they so often do. He had chosen to make the drinks as a good illustration of the principle he wanted the pupils to learn, and there was some shift in control here since they could choose their own ratio, make their own drink, and use their own ratio in the notes. The final shift would have been to use the material which the pupils had generated for the whole lesson, rather than move to material from the textbook, which was impersonal and unrealistic since all the ratios resulted in whole number solutions. None the less, this was a memorable lesson. Philip did not know exactly how it was going to go before he started, but he can now reflect and refine this activity so that much more of its learning potential can be exploited in the future.

7: How do you plan and evaluate lessons?

Student teachers, having observed an excellent lesson from a practising teacher without recourse to a single note, may be irritated by the requirement to produce written lesson plans in a teaching practice file. They may, however, be prepared to concede that they need to provide some sort of plan, so that the school mentors can keep a check that departmental plans are being followed, but balk at having to provide written feedback after the lesson. Such students say that they know how the lesson has gone and they don't need to write it down in order to reflect upon it. On the other hand, student teachers may feel unprepared for their first lessons unless armed with detailed notes of exactly what they are going to say, what the pupils will be asked to do, and practice examples worked out in full. Their first written lesson evaluations may act as a sort of emotional outpouring – a mixture of relief, pain, joy, perplexity and plans for the next day.

PLANNING IN THE EARLY STAGES

In the early stages of teaching practice, detailed written plans and evaluations can be an important form of support since the act of writing things down can be a good way of organising one's ideas but, perhaps more importantly, of encouraging reflection. Many inexperienced students will begin by concentrating on the mathematical content of the lesson, making sure they have worked through the mathematical activities beforehand. While this is useful, it is just not enough, as students will soon realise. Teaching mathematics is not about the teacher being able to do the mathematics, it is about providing pupils with opportunities to learn mathematics. So the teacher needs to have two models in her head:

1. the understandings and the experiences which the pupils will bring to the lesson and
2. the more sophisticated understandings she wants the pupils to attain.

Lessons can be seen as a delicate balance of assessment and teaching, the one dependent on the other. This requires a high degree of interaction between pupils and teacher, some of which can be planned in advance by addressing the question of how the lesson will take shape. In a comprehensive overview of the principles and the styles of lesson planning, Pat Perks and Stephanie Prestage (1994) point out the importance of not only having mathematical objectives but also planning lessons with an eye to other concerns:

- *Social –*   working in groups, pairs
                      listening to each other, sharing etc.
- *Control –*   starting, finishing the lesson
                      suitability of activities etc.
- *Cross-curricular –* use of IT, communicating verbally
                      writing a report, etc.

As an example, consider these lesson plans from a student on her first teaching practice (Examples 7.1–7.3). She had decided to write these up in her own way, but following the headings of a standard pro forma. This is a very sensible strategy, since it frees up students to write plans in the most helpful way to them, particularly when they are trying to keep several issues under consideration.

DISCUSSION

There are a variety of ways of looking at this set of plans and evaluations, and no doubt there are points on which more clarification would be helpful. I will, however, offer some of my own interpretations which the reader can consider in the light of the evidence. Firstly, the three lessons could be viewed as a whole – a story linked by Rachel's evaluations, in which she is finding her feet with a particular class. Without over-dramatising the situation, she has included some remarks from pupils which hit home to her and forced her to rethink her plans. In the end she feels that she has made the breakthrough she needs to continue more happily with them, and seems to fix upon the change in her questioning as a critical factor in her success. This leads her to make a resolution for future lessons:

> 'I shall work hard at trying to find open-ended questions where the ideas come from the pupils, not just my idea being forced upon them.'

The first lessons with a class will inevitably involve some negotiation between the mathematics, the pupils and the student teacher. Rachel has used her evaluations to identify weaknesses and identify alternatives, but there is also an emotional element to them, perhaps the most important part at this stage.

Breaking down the sequence of lessons into particular areas gives us an alternative analysis (Table 7.1).

Looking at the lessons with this breakdown gives us other insights which we can compare with the Perks and Prestage analysis. Most of the problems identified in the first two lessons appear to have been resolved in the third, and some of the difficulties are not mentioned again. It would seem that Rachel's major strategy has been to work on the suitability of her activities, from the *control* category of the analysis. This

Table 7.1 Analysis of progression over three lessons

Problem	Lesson 1	Lesson 2	Lesson 3	Strategy
Low motivation	Yes	Yes	No	Change topic and approach
Lack of challenge accessibility	Yes	Yes	No	Differentiation by outcome,
Differentiation	Yes	Some	No	As above
Timing	Yes		Some	
Chatting	Yes			
Noise	Yes			
Questioning	Some		No	Use an open ended question
Explanations		Yes		
Purpose lesson	Yes	Yes	No	Interest, link with Science
Textbook		Yes	No	Use it selectively

involved the choice of starting point, the form of questioning and the opportunities for matching within the mixed ability class. She makes passing reference to working in groups, a *social* consideration, as her aim in lesson 3 but it is not clear how this is planned for or achieved in practice. Her link with Science was planned for, as a justification for this particular topic, and so there is a *cross-curricular* dimension in the sense of linking with other school subjects.

At this stage in her progress, it is probably fair to say that the major priority for Rachel is in selecting and managing suitable classroom activities and that getting this right has been crucial in her relationship with this particular class. This is very typical of many students right throughout the year of training, not just in the early stages, and it is sometimes disappointing that they do not recognise the potential of their lesson planning to improve poor relationships and even problems of breakdown in control. Rachel's evaluations give us a very real feel for how her Year 7 class could have become disaffected, bored and frustrated if she had not reflected critically about her classroom activities, and in particular, how best she could access and channel the pupils' contributions.

Rachel's planning is fairly typical, but her evaluations are more lengthy, perceptive and constructive than those of many students including those in a later stage of their course. Although the proof of the pudding is in the eating, students like Rachel who consistently produce detailed written plans and evaluations are opening their practice to scrutiny, providing evidence of being prepared and have a record of what they have done if things go wrong. Students without this back-up are not only losing an opportunity to analyse and reflect in a deliberate way, they are taking a risk – if they have a bad lesson and there is nothing on paper, they will be open to criticism. As teachers become more publicly accountable, having recourse to such evidence is increasingly important.

Almost certainly, the school mentor and class teachers will give guidance about the topics to be covered and resources available. There may be some choice of topic

Example 7.1   Lesson one

Year 7 (mixed ability)   13 Nov 1995

Aim
To learn how to find factors.

Objectives
By the end of the lesson they should be able to identify what a factor is and how to find factors of a given number.

Pre-knowledge
Counting.

Introduction
Take the number 8. It can be represented in several different ways using dots.

```
    . . . .          . . . . . . . .        . .              .
    . . . .          1 x 8 = 8              . .              .
    2 x 4 = 8                               . .              .
                                            . .              .
                                            4 x 2 = 8        .
                                                             .
                                                             .
                                                             .
                                                             8 x 1 = 8
```

Pupils write these in their books.

What about the number 12?
Get pupils to suggest different ways of representing 12.

What about the number 7?
. . . . . . .1 x 7

Then get pupils to find factors of:
(i) 20   (ii) 18   (iii) 10   (iv) 11   (v) 27

What did the pupils notice about 1, 2, 4, and 8?
Get them to explain in their own words and then clarify it in a definition.

Factors
All the numbers which divide exactly into a number.

Conclusion
Ask the pupils how they know when they've found *all* the factors. Go through in a systematic way at any suggestion made by the pupils.

Now do
(vi) 9   (vii) 28   (viii) 24   (ix) 15   (x) 42

Evaluation

I was not happy with the way the lesson went. I did not maintain pupils' interest and motivation. The well-behaved ones did everything asked of them. Some of the cocky ones asked me what they were having to do dots for. I pitched the lesson at too basic a level. The lower ability pupils were happy doing dots, but hearing others saying that it was too easy, they too did not want to draw dots. Because some of the pupils found it easy they did the questions quickly. I had to draw conclusions too soon before the end of the lesson, and had to plunge into unplanned territory. They ended up at completely different stages by the end of the lesson. The work covered may have benefited the lower ability pupils but did nothing for the higher ability ones.

The lesson was noisy and a bit chaotic and I don't feel that any part of the lesson was particularly successful. However they did respond well to my questioning but I could have probed deeper into their mathematical thoughts.

For the next lesson, I will have to recap and move quickly on to ways of finding factors of numbers which are too large to do with dots and give them useful methods of finding whether a number is divisible by 3,4,6 and 9 without using a calculator.

Next time I shall endeavour to employ more authoritative strategies to deal with persistent chatting and senseless tale-telling.

Example 7.2   Lesson two

Aim
Seeing how factors can be obtained from a multiplication square and then more
practice on systematically writing down factors, working from the textbook.

Objectives
By the end of the lesson, they should know how to find all the factors of a given number,
larger numbers than before.

Pre-knowledge
Multiplication tables – even if they don't know, they can read off from a chart above the
white board.

Resources
Photocopy some exercises from book for homework.
Rulers.

Introduction
Who can remember what a factor is?
Then carry on from where they got to last lesson.
Most people were on a multiplication table.
e.g. Copy and complete   See p.133 exercise 4

x	1	2	3	4	5	6	7	8
1	1	2						
2	2	4	6					
3	3	6		12				
4				16				
5								
6								
7								
8								

Use your multiplication table square to find the missing numbers

$\boxed{1} * \boxed{?} = \boxed{10}$ $\boxed{2} * \boxed{?} = \boxed{10}$

What are the factors of 10?

Then find the factors of other numbers some of which aren't in the table.
If they finish this they can do exercise 6.
e.g. copy and complete

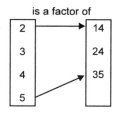

is a factor of

Conclusion
Some numbers are too big to read off tables or draw dots etc.

Homework
Class divided into 3. One set to investigate numbers divisible by 3, 4 and 9 in the form of:

Number	Divisible by . . . ?	Sum of digits

Evaluation

The lesson didn't really have an objective and just drifted along. The pupils seemed happier with working from a textbook, as this is what they're used to. However, there were still remarks about how boring endless factors was. I am inclined to agree.

*The pupils knew what they were doing and showed no real interest in the work. Again, I have to be tougher on the discipline side of things. The opportunities for differentiation were there only in as much as the higher ability pupils could try to find **all** the factors as opposed to the lower ability pupils finding only those factors that they could think of. I didn't present enough challenging material for the brighter ones. I didn't explain the homework very well either. I will leave more time to explain what is expected of them and create opportunities to ask me questions about it.*

I want to abandon this way of working and switch to sequences, using resources other than textbooks.

Example 7.3   Lesson three

Aim
Try to get them working as a group.

Objectives
By the end of the lesson they should have an idea about some kinds of sequences, that there may be more than one way of generating a sequence.

Pre-knowledge
Some knowledge of addition and multiplication.

Introduction
Pool results of homework.

2	is a factor of a number if the last digit is even.
10	is a factor of a number if the last digit is 0
5	is a factor of a number if the last digit is 0 or 5
3	is a factor of a number if the sum of the digits can be shared by 3

e.g. 948 sum is 9 + 4 + 8 =21 =3 * 7
21/3 = 7 whole number

4	is a factor of a number if the last two digits can be shared by 4
9	is a factor of a number if the sum of the digits can be shared by 9.

Working as a group.

Sequences: Important – it helps to understand scientific results
1, 2, 4 . . . How might this continue? Discuss:
1, 2, 4, 7, 11, 16 . . .
1, 2, 4, 5, 7, 8, 10, 11 . . .
1, 2, 4, 8, 16, 32, 64 . . .
1, 2, 4, 1, 2, 4, 1, 2, 4 . . .

What about 6, 8, 10, 12 . . . Add 2. . . multiples of 2 – quick definition depending on time.

Do you recognise these numbers?
1, 4, 9, 16 . . .

1 = 1   = 1 * 1   = 1
1 + 3 = 4   = 2 * 2   = 1 + 2 +1
1 + 3 + 5 = 9   = 3 * 3   = 1 + 2 + 3 + 2 + 1
1 + 3 + 5 + 7 = 16   = 4 * 4   = 1 + 2 + 3 + 4 + 3 + 2 + 1

1 + 3 + 5 . . . . + (2n-1) =
Different ways of representing square numbers.

What is the twelfth square number?
the twentieth?

Pg 147 Ex 23 Finish for homework.

Count regions

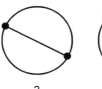

2   4   8   16   32

Pascal's triangle

Evaluation

I was much happier with the way the lesson went today. I spent a few minutes going over the homework so that things weren't left in the air and then I started a new topic which I felt more comfortable about teaching. My questioning was much more effective, in that it was left to them to decide what they thought the answer should be. Particularly the question, 'How might this sequence continue?' (1,2,4 . . .) – I had written in my lesson plan a few possible suggestions but they came up with those and about half a dozen more! I involved a few of the lower ability ones, drawing them in to the conversation, by encouraging them to draw the pattern if necessary. Everyone seemed full of ideas and eager to express them. In the future I shall work hard at trying to find open-ended questions where the ideas come from the pupils, not just my ideas being forced on them. The lesson was pitched at the right level for everyone it seemed because they were all interested and motivated enough, even when they then turned to the textbook to investigate more sequences – the very textbook they seemed bored by before! They seemed to understand what were patterns and sequences and what were not, judging by their ideas. I then asked them why they thought sequences were important – No answer. So I then asked what they were doing in their Science lessons and what did they do with their results and were they spotting patterns. Again they were bursting to tell – the lesson flew by and unfortunately the bell went before I had time to 'end' the lesson properly. However I won't be there for the next lesson so I have left them to get on with more sequences which I will go over next time.

By encouraging the pupils to explore and appreciate that, given a few numbers, there are many different directions that they can go in, they were given a more intuitive approach to investigating sequences. For example, as they were more aware of the different patterns that could occur, when given a set of sequences which did only have one answer, they were not stumped when the sequences went from adding the numbers, to multiplying the numbers, which I think they would have been if I had chosen a more closed approach.

There was a good working environment and I feel a lot happier about teaching this year class!

and approach, or the school may have very tight guidelines about what is to be taught and how. Both situations have advantages and disadvantages – too much choice can be frightening, too little can be stifling. The student needs to be clear about this. If a choice is being given then it is wise to share the plans with the mentor before teaching so that modifications can be made or more detail can be included. In the opposite case, the student really needs to check that this is so. Some teachers offer their own preferred approaches to be helpful, but this can sometimes be misinterpreted as a directive. Often the same teachers expect the student to show initiative and come up with alternatives as well.

In the new school-based courses, shared planning has enormous potential. The student could take the initiative here, by having some general written plans which could form the basis for a mentoring session well before the lesson takes place. Asking the mentor and other teachers how they would have planned the lesson and why, may also be very useful even if students intend to try out their own plans first. Some mentors have resisted offering their own preferred ways because they have not wanted to impose their ways of working on the students, but some are now beginning to realise the potential value of unpicking their own practice as a constructive way of moving students on and presenting alternatives. Ultimately the student will find his or her best way of planning, but 'discovering' this by repeated trial and error with little guidance may be a very inefficient method of learning.

USING A STANDARD LESSON PLANNING PRO FORMA

Whereas Rachel chose to plan her lessons in her own preferred way, many partnerships offer pre-planned pro formas, which have both advantages and disadvantages. Some students seem to need them as a form of organisation, but others find them restrictive. One of the advantages of a top sheet, whatever its form, is having a few really important points marked and available at a glance, but these should only be seen as an end point in planning. The earlier stages may well be messy and need redrafting, if real thought is going into this process.

In Example 7.4 a standard pro forma is used, and the evaluation follows a list of suggested questions provided by tutors to aid in post-lesson reflection. Also attached is an information sheet giving numerical information about the major bodies in the solar system.

The lesson planning here is quite brief but clear, although there is very little reference to how explanations etc. were going to be made. Probably the major factor in this planning was in thinking of a way to bring this topic to life. Similarly, the evaluation sticks to the suggested questions and offers little amplification. What does come over to the reader is the interest and motivation aroused by using the planetary data, so this is clearly an idea to be used in the future, perhaps with the limitations suggested.

Example 7.4 Lesson plan

Date 19/11/96	Class 10A1 Time Period 3 NC refs: AT3 L7
Aim(s)	Cover volume and surface area of spheres, do worksheet and possibly go onto mixed exercise in book. Get homework in.
Objective(s)	State formulae, give out worksheet for completion, start on book exercise.
Pre-knowledge	Pythagoras, area volume and perimeter formulae given in previous lessons (go over with absentees).
Resources	Vickers 9 & 10, STP 4A, worksheet and factsheet on planets, chalk and board (wet paper towel).
Timing	REGISTER VOLUME OF A SPHERE (formula, radius cubed, × approx. 3, × $1^1/_3$) SURFACE AREA OF SPHERE DENSITY = MASS/VOLUME IN SCIENCE YET? IN g/cm^3, or kg/m^3 REMIND OF STANDARD FORM – USING EXP PLANETS AREN"T PERFECT SPHERES BUT ASSUME THEY ARE AND ANSWER QUESTIONS ON SHEET (DON'T FORGET TO CHANGE DIAMETER) IF TIME – Vickers p208, no 5,7,9,10, p211, REVIEW 4 STOP 12.15 ANSWERS HOMEWORK IN – OTHERWISE STAY BEHIND – LUNCH

Solar system
1. What is the volume of Passiphae?
2. How much bigger in volume is Pallas than S14?
3. What is the surface area of Chiron?
4. If the surface area of Pluto is 31.2×10^6 km^2, what is its diameter?
5. What is the volume of the sun in m^3 ?
6. What is the density of the sun?
7. If the mass of the earth is 5.98×10^{24} kg what is the density of the earth?

Hint: use the volume of the sun to find the volume of the earth.

Evaluation

How did you feel at the end of the lesson?
OK, bit rushed

Did you achieve any of your aims and objectives? (or cover any you didn't expect)
Did introduction O.K., didn't finish sheet, went over m $\rightarrow$ m³, cm $\rightarrow$ cm³

Did you maintain pupils' interest and motivation?
They seemed to enjoy the sheet on the planets – had quite a few comments about how interesting the facts were

Was there an orderly working environment?
Yes, quiet talking

Did you pitch the lesson well?
Maybe a few too many things for them to think of – vols, std form, m³, cm³ etc. otherwise OK

Were there opportunities for differentiation?
If they work fast , Vickers

Were the timings right?
Yes, stopped every now and then to give answers – may have interrupted them

Was the questioning effective?
Sometimes, the quieter ones are reluctant to talk

Did the pupils understand the subject matter?
Yes – applied it well – had some problems with changing subject – I had a problem explaining

Which parts were particularly successful?
The worksheet

How do you know?
Comments

What would you do differently next time?
Some explanations – maybe do a few less things on the worksheet

Where do you go from here?
Finish homework and tackle problems

How could you assess pupils' progress?
Homework and going round to ask questions

The following evaluations are written in a more holistic way:

1.   'Lesson went fairly well. Each child produced diagonal patterns and stuck them in book. Had trouble with one girl with glue – too much – used some from hers for another girl's pattern. Table test at the end – very dubious. Most children said they had 9 or 10 right, which is a bit doubtful for the 7 times table.'

2.   'The pupils had already covered Venn diagrams, but I continued with the lesson plan as I felt it was a good lead in to looking at data handling. I think it worked well to use data that was of interest to the pupils. The class were a bit rowdy (first week after the exams, last lesson of the day). There was also some disruption as two pupils from other classes were sat in the classroom finishing a test. I think the pupils understood how to *interpret* Venn and Carroll diagrams but I do not believe they would think of using these themselves if presented with raw data.'

3.   'Most of the pupils needed more prompting than I thought they would. Most, if they did draw a table, wrote the values in in a random order and so couldn't see the link. Even when I got them to put the values on order, although they could see the pattern, couldn't turn this into a formula. Most also didn't try to write down anything they noticed until they asked me if it was reasonable first. The pupils therefore need much more practice with investigations and possibly a lesson on discovering formulae. The investigation did however fill in the 50-minute lesson well, but I obviously gave the class too much credit at being able to solve these investigations. It was, however, a very good problem because it made them think for themselves.'

Although each of these is brief, the encouraging thing about all of them is that there is some mention of the mathematics! This is an important element, but is often ignored in favour of comments about pupils' behaviour. Moreover, in 2 and 3, there are two very important teaching points:

- the difference between being able to understand a form of representation and the decision to choose it,
- the difficulty in moving from spotting number patterns to expressing them generally in a formula.

An alternative way of structuring evaluations is to write about the lesson in categories. This has the advantage of reminding students of the different aspects of a lesson and may encourage them to reflect in a more analytical way. The following gives an example of this type after a lesson about loci (Example 7.5).

PLANNING WITH MORE EXPERIENCE

As a parallel to the students' examples, I will now include my own written planning for a sequence of lessons with a year 6 class in a local primary school (Example 7.6). Coincidentally, the content of the lessons has something in common with Rachel's first topic of factors but the starting point is different. I did not know the pupils very

Example 7.5   Post-lesson analysis

Evaluation
A very enjoyable experience with a comfortable atmosphere. This has been a good week with 10X3. They have *all* done some good work with loci and I think the fact that it hasn't been too taxing mentally has understandably helped. I have been impressed with the change of attitudes in my 'gang of four' girls and they seem a lot more settled. Again I have started to be a bit more assertive with the class and I am now fully in control of who has done what homework etc. and this can only help the cause. I hope this improved relationship continues throughout my final fortnight as we cover Pythagoras.

Learning mathematics
The start of the lesson brought a construction of the Ellipse locus. I ran through requirements on the board and as the class developed the locus so many couldn't believe they had got it right. Where does this lack of confidence come from? The Tethered Goat worksheet was introduced without explanation and this time it was extremely refreshing to see the class having a go and getting it right. Most were perfectly happy they were right which was great to see. Reciprocating Rod worksheet set for homework (together with some textbook questions) was briefly explained. The words used probably make it look the most daunting but, in practice, it will be the easiest of all. I had to create a final locus where 'Suzanne' was tethered to a triangular hut in a field of money. Unfortunately we didn't have time to find out where she would be safe from the boyfriend.

Behaviour
Brilliant. The class were highly motivated and the working environment was great. AB commented about how nice the atmosphere in the room was.

Assessment
I feel it is only fair to say that good work has been produced by SG, WMcN & LP today. SW was absent. This was a refreshing contrast with previous straight line work. TC seems to be the worst in terms of lacking in confidence. She showed me her work each time I passed by, sure that she had not understood what to do. Each time she was actually spot on and I told her not to underestimate her ability. On the whole most of the class just wanted a congratulatory pat on the back and deservedly got one.

Time management
I had anticipated problems with the Tethered Goat example as there had been to some extent with all the other Loci. Someone always has a problem. When this didn't happen I was amazed and it left me with 10 minutes to fill at the end of the lesson. In my panic I created the 'Suzanne' problem which gave us all a laugh and I was disappointed not to finish it to be able to talk about loci regions. But I was pleased to have been able to think on my feet in that situation.

Example 7.6   Investigating rectangles

Resources
Squared paper (cm²), pencils, rulers, lined paper for write-up
Big sheets – grid
List of things to do in an investigation
Coloured stickers

Aims
To do some Ma1 work with a mixed ability class
Accessible starting point
Differentiate by outcome
Share results

Objectives
Pupils to see:
1. that you can draw several different shaped rectangles with the same area.
2. every area can be represented by at least one rectangle.
3. any area can be represented by a rectangle – the length and the width are factors of the area.
4. process skills – organising work, recording results.
5. general statements.

Lesson
Class sitting at tables:
1. Invite someone to come out and draw a rectangle on the large squared sheet, and find its area.
2. Everyone draw five rectangles on their squared paper. Swap with partner. Partner works out the number of squares inside each rectangle.
3. Share: mention area. Collect results randomly.
4. Make it systematically organised.
5. Talk about different shaped rectangles with the same area.
6. Give each table a pair of target areas. How many different ways, individually, then collect in group to report back to the whole class
   24, 17   25, 36   30, 40   16, 51

Write-up (after break):
 • What have you found out so far?
 • Can you write down what you have done so that someone else can understand it? Use squared paper so you can write and illustrate at the same time.
 • Compare with NC criteria

Challenges:
 • Are there any areas you cannot make?
 • If I give you a number, e.g. 864 could you find all the possible rectangles?
 • When would you know you had finished?

Evaluation

Lots of pupils had done rectangles of 24 cm² and this provided the opportunity to share and then list these systematically. This was going very well until Nick said 8 by 12 just after someone had given the 2 by 12 example. I tried to go through this on the board but I didn't labour it because I didn't want him to be embarrassed – I said I'd see him later to check. He sought me out later and showed me where the problem was – he had misread 84 cm² for 24 cm².

When they got onto the targets they started to tell me things they were finding out. I decided to be non-committal and write these findings up on the board.

Fiona and Leanne were very excited about 17 – 'there's only one way to do it.' I just wrote that up and didn't agree or disagree. In a few minutes they had decided to modify their finding to include halves and quarters in the dimensions.

I got into a bit of an argument with David, Andrew and Lee. They wanted to know if they could include squares so that they could do the area of 25 cm² as a 5 by 5 square. I just said that a rectangle only had to have right angles to be a rectangle, and left it up to them to decide if they could include squares. They wanted me to tell them whether to include squares or not.

When I showed them the bit from the NC to compare what they had done with what was written they went rather quiet. I don't know if this was because they had never been told what was in the NC before or if they did not understand some of the words and phrases e.g. make general statements . . . based on evidence they have produced, explain their reasoning.

Achievement of objectives
From the write-ups and observation:
- Everyone had evidence of several rectangles with the same area (obj 1).
- Implicit evidence from most pupils that you could always make a 1 by n rectangle (obj 2) but not explicit enough.
- Explicit evidence of using factors and/or using the word factor from 9 pupils out of 28 (obj 3).
- Laura is the only one who is completely at a loss when trying to draw a rectangle from its area. Unless it is very obvious or she can see someone else's work she does not have a strategy at all. This was a surprise and a worry. She must have a very limited feel for number, since she seems to keep drawing rectangles in the hope of hitting the required area.
- Some (but not conclusive) evidence of a general strategy. The five who did the challenge seem to be on the way here.

Interesting examples of pupils' work

Laura D:
'. . . I found out that there is only one way to make rectangle of 17 cm² without using halves and quters. I can only do 17 once because it only divides into itself and number one. 17 and 1 are the only two factors in 17.

'For 24 it was very easy because 24 had alot of factors. We did 4 × 6, 2 × 12, 1 × 24, and 3 × 8. When we started using fractions it got harder. We did 3/4 × 32, 1/4 × 96, and 3/8 and 64.'

Nathan:
'1. We all drew five rectangles in different ways. After that we swopt are papers with the person next to us. We had to work out they area of the of the rectangle. By working out we had to times it. Then we addit all up then when we get they answer then put it in the rectangle.
2. We found out that when we addedit all and when we done it came out as a paten.'

Tom:
'. . . Then we talked about it. We found out that 25 you could only do one unless you used halfs. We could of don it another way like 5 by 5 but that would turn into a square. On 17 you could only do it once unless you used halfs. This is because they don't go in tables.'

Fleur:
'CHALLANGE. 864 × 1, 432 × 2, 108 × 8.'

Ashley:
'. . . Next we made a chart and wrote all the different ways of making 24. We used whole numbers first then fractions. We looked for a pattern and found out that the widths were all in the 4 × table.'

Laura D:
'. . . Then we discussed the Area of 24 cm². There are four whole number combinations and six fraction number combinations. The numbers were all even except *3 × 8*.

	6 × 4	16 × 1 1/2
whole	8 × 3	4 × 4 1/2
	12 × 2	32 × 3/4
	24 × 1	96 × 1/4
		64 × 3/8
		192 × 1/8'

Edward:
Edward did not do a write-up. The next time I visited he presented me with three pages of fractions and working out:

'192 = 1/8
384 = 1/16
768 = 1/64'

and he continued this pattern until

'513460448 = 1/214748362
1027920896 = 1/4248704'

Discussion

The children's write-ups differentiate between those who see the task in a holistic way, and can describe and explain the underlying mathematical structure. Laura D falls into this category, whereas Nathan's write-up is very descriptive and does not present results or explanations. In one or two responses there is evidence of the pupils *looking for patterns* (Ashley and Laura D), and in Edward's case *using a pattern* to produce more cases. For some pupils the activity may simply have given them practice in finding the area of a rectangle.

The four pupils who successfully completed the 864 cm² challenge clearly had a strategy which they could apply to any given area. It seems to me that they were using factors here, even if they had not mentioned the word in their write-up, and that their method could be seen as the beginnings of generalisation.

General comments

I felt really good about this lesson, although the class seemed quite shy at first, and a bit wary of me. Getting them into the activity with plenty of specific things to do seemed to open them up and give them something to talk about. Those who came out to demonstrate their findings to the whole class did well on the whole although Mark stumbled when drawing 17 cm² with a 8 1/2 cm by 2 cm rectangle. I could feel a *frisson* of criticism from his group and he suddenly seemed to lose confidence in himself but he persevered with help. Nick was more buoyant today – he was noticeably uninvolved in the scheme work they were doing last week.

The class behaved very well and worked hard. I think this was partly because the activity lent itself to differentiation, partly because of the different groupings (pair, group, whole class sharing) and partly because of the novelty of having a different teacher. Several of them seemed genuinely excited by their discoveries.

Things for the future

- The issue of squares and rectangles, and the introduction of fractions seemed to take precedence over the factors idea, but I was pleased to follow these leads. Should I keep talk about having squares and rectangles for the start in future? Should I disallow fractions?

- The pupils needed a lot of help with the write-ups and I think I'd do more class and group discussion first in future. For this class I'll make a big display of their work to illustrate various features, e.g. explaining why something is happening, organising work systematically, etc.

- I would also change the targets for each table in future and give each table three targets – with a prime number and a square number in each set of three. It was noticeable that the pupils who had 17 wrote more about factors in their write-up, and the ones with 30 and 40 didn't mention factors, so I don't think I had given them enough of a chance with those numbers.

- I would need to do a lot more work before I could get some of them to make general statements. The challenge of giving a big number is worth repeating and pressing on with the question 'When do you know you've finished?'.

- Also, I'm going to use something like:

Quadrupeds are animals with four legs.

Cows have four legs and they also eat grass.

Is a cow a quadruped?

Rectangles have four right angles.

A square has four right angles and also has equal sides.

Is a square a special sort of rectangle?

- One girl who was interested in the fractions idea had developed a pattern idea from the easier fractions and wanted to know how to check this on the calculator. This is worth doing with more of them as it introduces the idea of the fraction as a division when converting it to a decimal. Fractions calculators?

- Finding factors using the calculator – there could be a very productive lesson here which would reinforce the meaning of factors and links between multiplication and division.

- Some one-to-one with Laura to see if she can make the connection between area and dimensions.

well, having only spent a morning helping in their classroom before this taught lesson. This provides a point of contact with myself and a student teacher, although clearly this is meant to be the planning of a more experienced teacher. Also, since I was not teaching as a regular teacher in the school I was more self-conscious of my plans and evaluations than if they had been part of my regular daily routine, so my thoughts are more open to analysis. In the evaluation, instead of writing a blow by blow account, I have included critical incidents and examples of pupils' work, plus some general comments. I will leave the reader to form judgements about the suitability of the planning, to think what they would do next, and to critically examine the interpretations which are woven into the writing.

Such an extensive evaluation is completely unrealistic after each lesson on teaching practice, but this one was done after an extended period of time on this task. Moreover, I was using the material with students as part of their course on lesson planning and evaluation, so my reflections were bound to be very explicit and detailed. As students become more experienced, however, it may be a good idea to do a detailed evaluation like this after a block of work, and to include a more detailed assessment analysis with examples of pupils' work.

CONCLUSIONS – PRINCIPLES IN PLANNING

The examples used in this chapter show the depth and complexity which can be involved in planning and evaluating lessons. In many ways it is a very individual process, much of it the result of mental musing and discussions with peers and experienced practitioners. When planning lessons or schemes, I find it useful to have three questions, parallel to those used by The Mathematical Association (1995), in the back of my mind:

- Why should the pupils do this?
- What should they learn?
- How can I manage the learning?

Why?

Even though we have a prescribed curriculum, teachers need to have some idea of the importance of its contents and be able to share this with pupils. Some mathematical ideas are of no immediate practical relevance but have intrigued and fascinated people throughout the ages. For instance, a short historical introduction to work with prime numbers may introduce pupils to the idea that mathematics is not simply a utilitarian field of study.

Pupils need to appreciate the big ideas of mathematics and why they have been important for mathematicians throughout the ages. When I watch pupils doing endless algebraic substitutions or changing the subject of the formula I do wonder why no-one seems to stress one of the really big ideas in algebra – that of generality. This idea can be illustrated with a simple example:

A call-out charge for a plumber is £20, and the rate per hour is £15, plus VAT at 17.5%. Find a general formula for the total charge, excluding parts.

A response in words such as 'multiply the number of hours on the job by 15, add 20, then multiply the answer by 1.175' is a perfectly good example of a general formula. Its symbolic forms, e.g.

$$T = (1 + 0.01v) (hr + c)$$

$$T = hr + c + \frac{v(hr + c)}{100}$$

could be investigated for equivalence and could be used to illustrate the idea of variables and of constants. This explicit treatment may well come after pupils have worked with such equations and formulae in problems and are familiar with them, but need to appreciate the significance of the ideas they are using. Less day-to-day formulae, e.g. $E = mc^2$, could also be used to illustrate the power of algebraic generality.

Similarly, in data handling the ideas:

- that data is collected to help us answer questions;
- that averages are numbers we can use to represent a larger set of numbers and help us to make comparisons;
- that the ideas of probability can help us to make decisions.

are fundamental, and may help us to frame our classroom activities accordingly:

- start a data handling lesson with a question of interest;
- start a lesson on averages with data from two classes for which there may be interesting comparisons;
- start a lesson on probability with a game which requires a choice to be made at the beginning. Repeat to see if the pupils are making better choices in the light of experience.

Other mathematical topics are very clearly of practical utility and everyday applications can and should be brought into the classroom to supplement textbook exercises which are often watered down, and sometimes do not adequately reflect the real-life situation. The student should start making a file very early on containing at least:

- a local bus timetable
- a train timetable
- a list of foreign exchange rates
- temperatures around the world
- sports results
- pages from catalogues
- a page from an A-Z of the area near to school
- a photocopy of a map of the locality

and should start to think of class activities in which they could be used.

Newspapers are a mine of information of direct relevance to the classroom, since extracts from newspaper articles incorporating quantitative ideas into the text can be used to illustrate the importance of numeracy as well as literacy. For example, in an article describing new research on lone parents commissioned by the Policy Studies Institute, Yvonne Roberts uses figures as an effective way of communicating complex information:

> 'The average age of the never-married mother is 25. Only 1 in 10 single mothers is under 20 now, but over half had their first child as teenagers. (Their own daughters have a one-in-four chance of repeating the pattern.) Britain has one of the highest rates of teenage fertility in the EC, but since the government set a target of halving births to teenagers by the millennium, figures have dropped significantly, by more than 10% a year.'

Discussing extracts such as these will involve pupils in the everyday activity of reading the newspaper and the mathematics will be seen as a tool with which to elicit meaning and significance from the information. The extract in question contains several mathematical statements which need thinking about, and they are embedded within an authentic context, unlike many textbook exercise questions.

It is not only applications which need to be highlighted. Other whys can be answered by reference to the skills or ways of working which the pupils will develop as a result of the activity, and it is perfectly acceptable to be open with pupils and say:

> 'I want to do this with you today to see if you find a rule that seems to work in this situation, to test it out and then to say why the rule works. These are important processes which are not just used in mathematics . . . .'

Moreover, there are personal attributes which can be developed in the mathematics classroom – perseverance, toleration, the ability to challenge unjustified assertions.

All of these reasons are valid and should inform planning, so that if you want to foster an appreciation of mathematics as a multicultural activity you will need to find some good activities which demonstrate this, if you want to encourage pupils to be tolerant of each other you have to set up situations where they will learn how to work with each other, if you want to illustrate the relevance of mathematics you cannot just say this is so – you will have to find examples.

What?

This is probably the easiest part and the one which can dominate planning to the exclusion of all else. Of course students should work through the mathematics themselves first, but there is a temptation to think of the 'what' as simply mathematical content. There are other equally important learning objectives in a mathematics classroom, e.g.:

- how to cope with being stuck
- how to organise their work

- how to ask questions
- how to explain why something is happening
- how to compare and evaluate different methods.

How?

Very simple variations in the way in which lessons are organised can result in dramatically different learning experiences. In the 'investigating rectangles' lesson described earlier, there were opportunities for pair and group work, and for different outcomes which could be pooled with the whole class. This variation of groupings can be a very effective way of breaking up usual ways of working, and of producing different versions of the same problem around the class.

Teaching approaches can also be planned to provide alternatives. In Rachel's lesson on sequences, an open question produced a hive of activity in finding different possibilities. In the probability lesson in the previous chapter, the theory developed out of considering whether the games were fair. In the mystic rose lesson, there was some direct teaching of how to find and measure the required angle, but this was done in the meaningful context of producing the mystic rose. Philip's lesson on ratios started with the practical task of making the drink to the required concentration. If there is one unifying theme here it is that of purpose. The pupils had a clear goal, apart from the learning of a new technique or concept, but some of them also learned or reinforced new mathematics in the course of doing the activities. So in deciding how to teach, the student needs to look out for different approaches which will engage pupils in purposeful and meaningful activities. This is an ongoing process since building up a repertoire is a lifetime's work, but by keeping your interest fresh you will enrich your own learning.

Thirdly, student teachers need to plan for interaction. Careful thought is needed about:

- how to find out what pupils already know. Asking them if they can do equations is not very helpful – giving them a specific example will be.
- exactly what questions to use, and how they can be rephrased.
- how to use pupils' knowledge, suggestions, and examples.
- how to respond to errors. Moving on to someone else may be a lost opportunity.
- giving pupils something simple to do which will give them something to talk about straightaway, e.g. 'I want everyone in the class to fold their piece of A4 paper twice and to look at the shape you have made'.

Again this consideration of how to manage interactions will not happen overnight. It can only be done effectively after reflection, noticing lost opportunities and deciding how to react differently in future.

Sharing expectations is a very good idea. This may simply be an outline of the lesson, or the next few lessons. Or it may be expectations of pupils' behaviour, or how you want them to present their work, e.g. 'Do it in rough first, then we'll talk about it and then you can write it up later', or how you expect them to select and use the resources. Then, having set up expectations, remember to acknowledge success as well as failure.

Finally, beginnings and endings are important. The beginning may simply be an outline of the lesson and the ending may be some carefully chosen questions as a recap. At the end of one lesson I observed, a PGCE student asked the pupils what they had learned during the lesson, and gained a valuable insight into the lesson from the pupils' responses. Also look out for good starters, and do not forget that you can always end a lesson with something completely different – a short game, or some mental work, or a visualisation exercise. In some of the endings I have observed, pupils have done more mathematical thinking in a few intense minutes than they have been doing in the whole lesson.

How teachers teach reflects their personal philosophy, their views on and enthusiasm for mathematics, their relationships with pupils, and their willingness to learn alongside their pupils. It is a fascinating human study, so much so that Mathematics Teaching devoted a whole issue to this topic in June of 1992. Here we have the stories of academics, classroom teachers and PGCE students. It is well worth reading.

REFERENCES

Perks, P. and Prestage, S. (1994) 'Planning for learning,' in *Mentoring in Mathematics Teaching*, B. Jaworski and A. Watson (eds). Lewes: Falmer.

The Mathematical Association (1995) 'Why? What? How?' *Mathematics Teaching, Special Issue 'How I Teach'*, **June**.

8: Feedback, review and self-evaluation

LESSON OBSERVATION

Every mathematics lesson is an extremely complex event – even short extracts of video from lessons can provoke rich and lengthy discussions from practising teachers who may either focus upon different aspects of the lesson or try to weave together all these different aspects into a coherent interpretation. Observers are doing many things at the same time – trying to follow the action, watching the teacher, watching the pupils. If a student is being watched they may also be making judgements about the performance and the sort of feedback which may be helpful after the event. In the case of the student, there may also be a range of expectations of this feedback. The student may expect a judgement, or may be eager for advice, or may want their own voice and opinions to be a priority. Striking the right balance here may be difficult. If advice is given but the student feels powerless to disagree, there is a chance that good advice will be rejected and that resentment may set in. On the other hand, if the observer simply says that the lesson was fine, the student may feel let down and disappointed that an experienced practitioner cannot give some more constructive comment.

GETTING THE BALANCE RIGHT

In the following transcript of an oral feedback session after a lesson in the first practice, these tensions are clearly in evidence. The lesson began with pupils drawing triangles, tearing off the vertices and sticking them down at a point to lie on a straight line. A similar activity was then done starting with a quadrilateral. Once the two results were established the student gave the pupils two sequenced worksheets in which they had to find missing angles using the results.

> *Tutor:* So how do you feel it went?
> *Student:* . . . em drawing the shapes, cutting them out . . . took a lot longer than I thought it would and I had to go round everybody and say again that . . . which in a way was my fault because I wasn't clear enough in the first place but in a way I was as clear as I thought I had to be . . . so I don't know, I don't know.

Tutor: (This)

Student: (The homework was a bit too hard . . . .)

Tutor: What would you do . . . how would you change it . . . you'd make your instructions about sticking the shapes down more clear in the future, yes?

Student: (Yeah.)

Tutor: You reckon that this homework was a bit hard?

Student: It might have been.

Tutor: . . . and I think I'd agree with you there . . . What would you do to help them with that?

Student: Maybe do the first two with them and say how I'd worked out a and b and then maybe give them one of the next two and then let them fend for themselves . . . .

A little later in the interview, an alternative way of handling the angle sum is suggested:

Tutor: . . . and when you'd got the quadrilateral angles if you'd have said, if you'd have made a bit more about that complete turn bit, you know because you'd got the result that it was 360, and it might have been nice to say it's a complete turn.

Mentor: Yes, I'd put down just in general there that I felt the punchline was gone too quickly . . . it was just almost in passing that they came to 360 degrees and . . . just in the matter of presentation the challenge to disagree with the teacher when you are only Year 7.

(Laughter)

Mentor: (in a stagy voice) Does anybody disagree? (Laughter) No, right we're going on . . . and I don't know if . . . there was a lad sat right next to me who didn't have that and I felt . . . .

Student: Well . . . Well, how else do you deal with that?

Mentor: Well, I think I might . . . If I'd have been doing it I would have come at it slightly differently and I've had got them all to come out with their bits – there's a board here and have a stapler handy and say come and bang it on the board and get them all up and see if we could get a . . . something general established, not from everybody's but say well generally . . . and one or two people will have made a mistake . . . so generally it looks like . . . .

Student: One of the first things I said to the class last week was I'm not always right, I make mistakes sometimes, so if anybody thinks I've done something wrong tell me, and the next lesson I did make a mistake which somebody picked up on and a few times people have stopped in the middle of the lesson and said I think that's wrong and somebody even brought his paper back to me and said 'you've given me too many marks'. He counted them up again.

Tutor: Hmm, yes, but I think that that's a nice idea of N's to have them all up.

Student: Yeah.

Tutor: Because for a start off this is not a proof that the children have been given . . . it's a 'this looks as though it works in a lot of cases' sort of thing plus the fact that it's bound to be inaccurate because they are doing it practically, aren't they . . . they're drawing with rulers, they're cutting out, there are lots of opportunities for making errors and so I think it's important for them to see if they have made a slight error that's all in the nature of doing practical work . . . but it looks as if . . . it's working . . . and maybe just leave it at that.

Towards the end of the interview, the tutor and mentor review the main points:

Tutor: At the beginning when they were giving you answers you didn't sound very pleased with them, later on it was nice because you started to say very good and you must work on that because they're a lovely class and they really will respond to that . . .

Mentor: Yes, funny I've written that the child who said that there were 360 . . . that the angles of a quadrilateral added up to 360 degrees, that very first answer you seemed very upset that he got it, to be quite honest.

Tutor: Yes, you said 'Do you *know* the answer?'.

Tutor: I would have quite liked you to say 'How do you know that? How did you work that out?' You know, rather than Oh God he knows the answer – make more of it – I think there is always a tendency for you to supply the answers, OK (laughter) instead of dragging it out of them kicking and screaming.

Mentor: You're copying my notes.

Tutor: Yeah? (laughs) OK . . . . *You* gave a dictionary definition of a triangle, I would have quite liked them to come up with it because the tripod was really nice . . . much better to ask them what they noticed – that was with the straight line – You *told* them and again when you had got all the angles at the point this girl at the back was *bursting* to tell you that it was a complete turn you know . . . and then you tell her, I felt it was such a shame you know because she was going to tell you all sorts of interesting things . . . and I feel with her that if you don't give her some attention she might get a bit . . . irritable . . . .

The emphasis in this discussion changes from one in which Steven's recollections of the lesson are invited and developed, to one in which the tutor and the school mentor take a dominant role. Not surprisingly, Steven moves into the defensive, and tries to justify his actions. He appears to misinterpret the important lead that the mentor is giving him about how to handle a result which could only ever be approximate given the activity in question. Later on, the tutor and the mentor were clearly concerned that Steven was not using the class's responses enough and that he was ploughing on with the results he wanted them to accept and then use. Ironically, they fall into the same trap themselves – whereas Steven was supplying all the answers for the pupils, the analysis of the lesson was also one sided.

The difficulty here is a common one in mentoring. Steven needed moving on. He needed to move away from the superficial aspects of his lesson, to focus more upon the pupils and their learning. Whether he was ready or receptive for the advice he was given is doubtful, and the transcript illustrates this vividly. The tutor and mentor had decided that he needed a challenge, but Steven did not respond well to this. In the written feedback advice was summarised:

- You need to work hard on questions which draw out responses from the pupils.
- You need to stress the important points.
- You need to think carefully about sequencing and progression.
- Otherwise, very promising.

In his own responses to these comments, Steven wrote that they were fair, but of a later lesson observed by the school mentor he complained that:

> 'It seems that I am not allowed to criticise the children's efforts, yet my efforts can be criticised by teachers. I find this a difficult classroom to work in.'

Clearly, feedback after lesson observations is sensitive. Tutors and mentors need to be diplomatic, but students need to be able to accept and evaluate constructive criticism if progress is to be made. The fine balance between challenge and support needs to be maintained, and one of the ways this can be done is for the student to ask for future observations to focus upon weaknesses that have been identified and for strategies to be planned jointly. Discussion like this can usefully take place in periodic review sessions, when some time has elapsed after observed lessons and cooler reflection has taken place.

WORKING WITH THE STUDENT'S CONCERNS

In the second feedback session, the student had asked the IHE tutor to stay behind to talk about another class, not the one which had been observed. She starts with her problem:

> *Student:* . . . well we've had two good lessons . . . the first lesson was appalling it was a total disaster . . . they'd just come out of a maths exam and it was last lesson in the afternoon . . . and I think probably that frightened me to start with, you know I thought oooh . . . because they were all horrible, you know, not just naughty . . . they were just . . . they're bright enough kids and I think that they think ooh let's be really nasty to her because I'm young and they do go on about my age and ask how old I am and how long ago I was doing this at school and things . . . .
>
> *Student:* The first lesson I had with them I came out and I thought right that's it I'm going home and I'm not coming back.
>
> *Tutor:* Oh no.
>
> *Student:* (laughing) which is the first time I've thought that and so it was a bit of a shock because everything had just been swimming along nicely so I

suppose it was about time I got a shock.

Tutor: It can be like that and that's the thing about teaching, that it can feel very personal.

Student: Yeah, it does.

She then has the opportunity to say exactly how she feels about it before the tutor starts to offer some advice, both in terms of the student's mental attitude to the group and in terms of her expectations of their work:

Tutor: So OK you know this is where your grit has got to come in em and you're goin to have to er hang on in there . . . I would suggest that psychologically you need to refocus your attention in that group instead of . . .

Student: (Looking at the bad ones.)

Tutor: (Looking at the bad ones.) You've got to start to focus on the people who are potentially on your side, who may not be very influential within the group but . . . .

Tutor: OK, well I would really go for the work, the expectations that they are going to do the work, mark their work em and expect high standards because I think that may be something that you can use.

but in fact the student has already thought about the work and has started to solve her own problem in her lesson planning:

Student: Yes, we're going on to enlargements today, starting a new topic em and I've got both the exercises ready and everything and hopefully they'll catch on to it , scale factor and what not, but . . .

Tutor: Have you got an accessible starting point?

Student: Well one of the books that I've found, it starts just with say a drawing of a car, and it gives you measurements, dimensions, and it says 'if we enlarge this by a scale of 4 then how long would all of these things be?' so I think we'll start with that and then we'll go on to drawing triangles.

Student: . . . and I don't know how they'll feel about it but me I'd find it easier to make a car bigger.

The upshot of this conversation was that the student immediately had a successful lesson with the troublesome class, and began to develop a relationship with them. At the end of the course she described how she had achieved this:

'My best route to gaining confidence and involving them in the lesson . . . was to make the work more interesting for them, I think that I had a bit of a mismatch between the work and the group, we had been doing scattergrams for the first couple of weeks and they hated it, and my tutor said start something new, you can always come back to scattergrams, do something that is really going to get them involved, something that is going to last a while and they are going to have to think about, mark their work every 10 minutes if you can, put comments on it and challenge them, and I did.

'Yes, and I think that was a really good piece of advice. Whenever I've had trouble with my groups, I've made sure that they have had a target, a real definite target, you must complete this by the end of the lesson and it works.

'I think that one thing I've found out . . . is that children work better if they know exactly what they've got to do, when they've got to do it and that you're not going to tolerate any nonsense from them.'

Although this student seemed to find the discussion with the tutor very helpful there are some dilemmas here. Working on planning is clearly very important, and offering pupils stimulating mathematics should make a great difference, but the balance between planning for control and planning for learning is delicate. It is possible to establish control and in so doing remove opportunities for learning, making pupils submissive and imitative, which is where this student seems to be moving, judging by her final comments in the interview. My advice may have been a lifeline but it may have pushed her too far along this very directive route.

CHALLENGE ACCEPTED

Student: That was last week . . . I came out and I wasn't happy that the kids had understood it and I wasn't happy with the way I'd taught it . . . and I came out and I said to Mrs H what do you think of it about it . . . and she said I think there's too much language . . . but I'd thought . . . well they're not used to me . . . I'll have it all written down . . . this and this and with a mixed number I'd written fraction left over and I wasn't happy with that and I came out and thought that'd be all right if I was doing improper to mixed cos left over gives you a sense of division . . . you know a remainder sort of thing . . . I came out and I thought it's not really applicable to mixed numbers going to improper cos there's nothing left over . . . it's attached on to the mixed number so it was like oooh so I spoke to Mrs H and she said well get rid of a lot of the language get the kids just doing it . . .

Tutor: What interests me is why they are doing that work at all.

Student: Cos they're a Year 8?

Tutor: Go on.

Student: Do you think they're a bit backwards from what they should be . . . is it a bit easy?

Tutor: . . . No that's not what I feel . . . I'm asking why do we teach children about how to change improper fractions into mixed numbers and mixed numbers into improper fractions.

Student: Mmm, (laughing), apart from it being in the scheme of work . . . It's in . . . I was just told you're going to teach fractions and you're starting from here and I did a section on the language of fractions . . . how to say it and how to put it in words . . . I had a whole lesson on the language of fractions . . . I had them writing them out in words and then in figures so I did that and it made today's lesson a bit easier . . . I then lapsed into the equivalent fractions . . . the one thing I can say is that it does help with addition and what not . . . .

Tutor: but I just have this question mark and I think you should think about it . . .

Student: . . . and I haven't, that's the first time I've actually thought about it.

Tutor: So where do we . . . I'm going to put that down here . . . where do we use these mixed numbers and improper fractions in mathematical problems?

Student: Mm . . . .

Tutor: That's a little one for you to be pursuing and thinking about.

Student: Yea, that's a valid point, certainly . . . .

Student: I had planned a little activity at the end where they could find fractions in the real world . . . hopefully for next week I'll get something on that . . . I'll put that on my scheme because these kids have been sat there for weeks doing these fractions . . . .

Tutor: And if you look in the NC at how fractions move up they do start with very realistic things like find a fifth of a piece of wood which is so long . . . Finding fractions of things . . . and in fact if you look I think you'd be surprised at the level at which operations in fractions actually comes . . . the reason why I'm saying this is because it's quite easy to teach children this sort of thing.

Student: Yea?

Tutor: By rote.

Student: And that has been OK.

Tutor: But whether or not they can transfer it into a context or whether or not they've got a deep understanding . . . .

Student: . . . remains to be seen.

Tutor: So you're not fooling yourself.

Student: No, so that's what I can see next week because I'm going on to the 'of' factor.

Tutor: . . . those are the more important things that you'll need for percentages and things . . . so you'll need to probe understanding in different contexts . . . it might have been nice, I don't know if you noticed you did two questions on the board . . . was it 8/2 and 16/4 . . . it might have been nice to say we've got two different questions here and they've both given us the same answer . . .

Student: I could have drawn them back to their equivalent fractions.

Tutor: Yes, or could you have asked them to draw you a picture.

Student: I should've . . . it was just coincidental that I picked this one but I should have read into it a bit more . . . I realised it was giving the same answer but I hadn't thought of maybe tying it all together . . . .

Tutor: . . . just a little point about the test at the end . . . these were all written in that way . . . if you really want to probe children's understanding . . .

use a variety in your questions . . . and then I don't know if you noticed you said 'write down 12 over 24 in its simplest form' and then the same language again, '24 over 36', and then again '11 over 2, 4 over 3, 12 over 4', so you could have said 'write down twelve quarters as a whole number, write down 4 divided by 3'.

Student: That would have been a nice one cos we've worked a bit on that so I should maybe have done that . . . .

Tutor: another thing you might like to think about is which of these fractions is the biggest . . . and another one is where is this fraction on the number line . . . .

Student: . . . right.

In this lesson, a very confident and intelligent student had been teaching pupils a technique for changing mixed numbers into improper fractions, and I was frankly dismayed because the mentor had thought it was a very good lesson. I wanted her to go beyond this rote learning to develop meanings and connections and to think of contexts in which the knowledge could be used. This student was very receptive to constructive advice and responded to it. At least part of this advice had stuck because at the end of the course she observed that:

'Well the one bit about contextualisation that was given to me in the diagnostic practice has stuck with me . . . that one was about fractions and you're plugging away at fractions and you don't think to stop and tell to the kids . . . well here's something where we see these in real life . . . you know you're getting through the material . . . and I've been even more aware of this when I've taught the 'A' level students and I've taught them calculus and rather than plodding through tons of differentials and stuff I've stopped and a few examples of where we see it, a few practical experiments, which was nice, using the graphics calculators so I've definitely been more aware . . . and I think . . . I don't know if I would have been as aware had she not said it because it hadn't been given to me in the first practice . . . .'

WRITTEN FEEDBACK

The form of written feedback can be varied. There are usually official observation schedules but these may be preceded by the use of unstructured lesson notes. The lesson notes themselves may be written in a factual and non-judgemental way, with the observer writing what the student does and says and noting pupils' responses which the student may not notice:

'. . . Reminder about angles all adding up to 180 degrees.
You now set them off drawing the equilateral triangle of side 10 cm.
Kevin knew the angles would still be 60 degrees – because it was still an equilateral triangle. Craig's explanation was nice – you're just keeping the top the same and stretching the sides down. Steven thought the angles would be 100 degrees in this bigger triangle, before measuring to confirm 60 degrees.

You: Does anyone know what the midpoint is?

Pupils: middle.

Pupils all marking in points and joining them to form a new equilateral triangle.

You: How many new triangles?

How many altogether?

Steven had done another midpoint – he said he had 7. He was only counting the distinct triangles.'

or the observer may include judgements, hints or alternative ways of doing things:

'. . . You talked about the number of multilink in layers, referring to the drawing on the board. I would have done this from the 3D model personally. One girl told you it was l × b × h from your diagram – only two had their hands up at this point. It may have been worth reinforcing, instead of going straight on to notes.

'. . . you moved on to talk about the units of volume – you were getting at cm² – you need *centicubes* available at this point.

'Then you did a worked example on the board – find the volume of a brick 22 cm long, 8 cm high, 10 cm long. While you were writing it up on the board one or two were getting restless.

'You wrote up the working for them. You need to ask round the class first and do it together. The answer was 1760 cm³ – you asked them for a better unit – they gave you litre . . . It was nice when you linked this to the fruit juice carton and compared the sizes. Have the fruit juice carton there and use it rather than just talk about it – they could measure the dimensions and check out the volume . . . .'

Each method has its own advantages. With the first method, reading through the notes together after the lesson may give the student a good opportunity to give his own interpretations, to offer his own reasons for decisions taken and to identify weak points himself. The observer may guide the process of self evaluation in this way and hold back from giving his own judgements. The second method is useful because time is invariably short and students want to know what the observer thinks of the lesson. If there is advice to be had from an experienced teacher they would like it as soon as possible, rather than trying to reinvent the wheel themselves. Much will depend on the students' own preference for feedback, the stage in the practice and the judgement of the tutor or mentor. In the second of the two extracts above, the student was nearing the end of the second practice and the observer was giving specific examples of weaknesses which had already been identified and which the student was failing to address.

Any official pro forma for observation will be lacking and will need modifications as the partnerships develop, but there are advantages in having some consistency in the form of feedback even if the interpretations and emphases will inevitably vary from teacher to teacher. Some teachers are so pressed for time that they fill this in during the lesson as it progresses, others will complete this in discussion with the students at the end of the lesson and in some cases students will be invited to fill in one of these for themselves using their own recollections and the observer's running notes to help them reconstruct the lesson.

ALTERNATIVE PERSPECTIVES

In the following extracts, the focus is on one lesson taught by a student nearing the end of his main practice. In this lesson the student was introducing the class to a straightforward mathematical investigation to prepare them for the sort of activities they would be doing next year for their GCSE coursework. As such, it was a self-contained task and the outcome was to be a write-up of the investigation, following the criteria which would be used for assessment. It was a very unfamiliar way for them to work, although the student did refer to investigational work in science at the beginning of the lesson.

The investigation was called 'Cutting up a pizza', and the main aim was to find a generalisation for the maximum number of pieces formed by n cuts of a circular pizza.

1 cut – 2 pieces   2 cuts – 4 pieces   3 cuts – 6 pieces   **or**   3 cuts – 7 pieces

At the beginning of the lesson, the student wrote up and talked through the guidelines for writing up the investigation:

1. Write out the problem in your own words.
2. Do simple cases first.
3. Draw diagrams.
4. Write down what you are going to do as you go along.
5. Be systematic.
6. Draw a table and fill in as you go along.
7. Spot patterns and predict.
8. Look for general rules.
9. Explain why the pattern works.
10. Check or prove that the rule always works.

Extra marks are given for parts 9 and 10.

Readers may like to try the activity, and do their own write-up before continuing.

After the lesson there was a relatively short three-way discussion, largely led by the IHE tutor with input from the mentor. In the following sections, various perspectives on the lesson can be glimpsed. First, a transcript of the short oral feedback session is given. Then the student's own version (Figure 8.1) of the observation schedule is given, and finally the university tutor's (Figure 8.2).

Post-lesson discussion

Tutor: Well I must say I enjoyed it .

Student: They all seemed to be . . . doing OK didn't they?

Tutor: Yes . . . and it was lovely the way they . . . you kept on reminding them of the things you had said at the beginning and you kept on saying *write it down write it down* you know if you do a pattern . . . if you do a table you might be able to spot a pattern better . . . I thought it went well . . . .

Student: Did you?

Tutor: Really good . . . and particularly because it is obviously not an easy class.

Student: (Laughs.)

Mentor: No they're hard work.

Tutor: Absolutely.

Mentor: They're a rewarding class because you can get a tremendous amount out of them.

Student: Yes that's it and it's funny because I've only got about a week and a half left of them and em it seems I'm just about getting my way with them.

Tutor: Which is . . . it sometimes takes as long as that . . . it was lovely to see the work they were doing because M (the mentor) warned me that they might be quite reluctant to do something different . . . you said they were very happy to do textbook stuff.

Mentor: Oh yes.

Tutor: But they were quite capable of doing this and right from a very early stage some of them. (predicting)

Student: It helped that Stephanie wasn't in.

Mentor: Yes because she would be . . .

Student: Although even she might have been OK with this.

Mentor: I think she would have been . . . I mean it's these three boys.

Tutor: . . . but those are really a handful those three – it was quite funny because I thought oh my God those three and then very near the end I went and looked at this boy's work and it was quite good.

Student: Mark.

Mentor: That's the amazing thing, all of them are very good.

Student: They're some of the better ones in the class . . . Dean is.

Mentor: Dean is probably one of the best in the class.

Tutor: But they'd never show it would they?

Chorus: Oh no. (inaudible comments and laughter)

Tutor: These are some of my running commentary notes . . . I wondered at the beginning if this was going on too long.

Student: I was worried that it was because normally if I . . . (inaudible)

Tutor: Yes, but you just held it.

Mentor: Yes.

Student: I did the last two quite quickly I thought they were about to drop away.

Observation schedule

Class: 9 Set 2   Date/Time: Room:
Topic: Introduction to investigations and coursework (Ma1)

A Knowledge of the subject (competencies 2.2.1–2.2.3)
2.2.1.Good emphasis on concepts and skills in addition to basic knowledge.
2.2.2 Evidence of understanding AT1 SoA's in explanation of how different aspects of investigation (e.g. communication skills) contribute to overall skill in using and applying mathematics.
2.2.3 No obvious evidence, but pizza isn't mentioned explicitly on the curriculum.

B Application of subject knowledge (2.3.1–2.3.7)
2.3.1 Lesson plan based around Ma1 and fitting in with school's scheme of work.
2.3.2 New topic so continuity not an issue but fitted in with Science AT1.
2.3.3 + 2.3.4 Lesson was designed to keep their attention while explanation of investigation skills was done and did not expect them to listen for too long. Open-ended work allowed differentiation by outcome.
2.3.5 + 2.3.6 Strong emphasis on communication skills and language.
2.3.7 No IT in this lesson.

C Classroom management/organisation (2.4.1–2.4.4)
2.4.1 Cooperative individual work can be noisy but allows for useful collaboration developing communication skills as well as individual improvement.
2.4.2 Knew pupils' names – handled Gary when arguing about collecting books. Dealt with class distraction well. Good clean end to the lesson.
2.4.3 House points for James for good predictions and checking. Lots of praise for pupils who were getting the ideas.
2.4.4 Pupils remained on task for most of the lesson.

D Assessment/recording of pupils' progress (2.5.1–2.5.5)
2.5.1 No evidence – will be marked later.
2.5.2 No evidence – will be marked later.
2.5.3 No evidence – will be marked later.
2.5.4 Good awareness of pupil response to work allowing lesson to be adjusted accordingly. Also formative assessment for advice to individual pupils.
2.5.5 Report back to pupils at end of lesson with encouragement and praise; also saying where this would be leading next lesson.

E Relationships with pupils (2.6.4–2.6.8)
2.6.5 some pupils in this class (e.g. James) clearly have strong connection skills and others are capable of working very quickly. Need to account more for this.
2.6.7 No evidence but *this* is my self assessment.
2.6.8 No particular evidence but then M & S development is implicit, not explicit, in the majority of cases.

F Competencies requiring further development 2.2.3, 2.3.7, 2.6.5, 2.6.8
This was quite a good lesson so I was pleased with it. Obviously my competence in all the above can improve but I feel that I am going in the right direction and am quite pleased with my own progress.

Figure 8.1 Andrew's version (using the schedule for post lesson evaluation)

A This was an investigational activity which involved elements of AT1 (communication, reasoning) and AT3 (making and testing generalisations).

B The investigation was presented clearly and pupils were given several examples to familiarise themselves with the problem and direction to be followed. It was accessible, and provided opportunities for differentiation by outcome. Excellent opportunities given for pupils to explain things in their own words and develop their communication skills. Some very good work produced. Alternative ways of recording encouraged.

C Pupils were working either in pairs or in groups, but did their write-ups individually. A lively group, handled firmly, without losing their interest. Motivation increased noticeably as pupils became more involved in the work and achieved success.

D The assessment criteria for the work were shared with the pupils at the beginning and referred to as you circulated and monitored progress. 'Write that down etc.' You listen to the pupils and try to move them on without being over-directive.

E Good working relationships with the pupils. You are firm, open and reasonable with them. You encourage them and praise them for good work. You are obviously sharing in and enjoying their learning and progress.

F This was a very good lesson. With work like this you will need to develop the hard part - encouraging pupils to explain *why* their pattern/generalisation works.

Figure 8.2 Tutor's version

Tutor: I could see why you were doing it like that so you could talk it through as you were going.

Student: I thought about writing it up beforehand but if I'd done that they'd have all copied it down and I couldn't have explained it and they wouldn't admit.

Tutor: Yes I could see what you were doing and it worked.

Mentor: If you gave it on a sheet it would be the same.

Student: Yes.

Mentor: They wouldn't listen.

Tutor: I mean something you might do another time having done this way is actually to cut things out and ask them to reorder them and see in what order they have actually done the things you have suggested because in many ways actually writing out the problem in their own way is quite a hard thing to start with and sometimes you might ask them to work it through and then go back and try and explain.

Student: I find it helpful to have that first to give them practice using words.

Another member of staff enters, indicating that the room is needed.

Tutor: Well that's fair enough.

Discussion

Although I had some reservations about the form of the lesson, it seemed much more important to offer Andrew general praise and encouragement at the end of the lesson. He had tried something different with a lively class, and had worked hard throughout to encourage the pupils to take some initiative within a structured framework. Moreover, the pupils were more purposeful and engaged in their work than in any of the other lessons seen, and the write-ups, almost without exception, were very promising. Entering into a debate about the value of an investigative approach as opposed to doing a one-off investigation did not seem appropriate at the time. It was also clear that Andrew felt buoyant at the end of the lesson and the tutor was pleased to share in this happy state. Attempts to look in more detail at the structure of the lesson were cut short by the interruption. It was not possible to continue at that point and it was felt that it was more important for Andrew to do his own evaluation in the form of the observation schedule and then to compare it with my version.

The comments on both the observation sheets have many points in common, although Andrew has chosen to go through the competencies one by one, rather than make general points under each heading. He is clearly pleased with the lesson, and with his progress. In my feedback, I have tried to summarise the positive aspects of the lesson and to give him a pointer for the future. The last comment is really very important, and there is no indication in Andrew's writing that he has yet considered this, although it may well have been in his thoughts. If I had been the mentor, I would have wanted to see the planning and execution of this next lesson so that I could see if the pupils had made some progress in the development of their reasoning skills.

These are some of the questions I would have liked him to pursue:

- How do you know where to place the cuts to get the maximum number of pieces?
- What patterns can you see in your results?
- How many pieces would you get with 50 cuts? Why? Is there a general rule?
- Why does it work? What is it about the cuts and the pieces that makes it work?

I would have also liked Andrew to spend some time going over the suggested sequence and seeing how the pupils' ways of working had matched up to this. In many ways, although a lot of time by Andrew, myself and the mentor in analysing this lesson, the job has only really been half done, and Andrew's ability to make the best of future lessons like this will depend a great deal on opportunities and critical support in his first post. But knowing how much a student can usefully take on board is critical, and bombarding him with advice is probably less important at this stage than encouraging him to find his own voice.

Interestingly, Andrew made some comments about these issues in his end-of-course interview:

Interviewer: What about [the written] feedback? What did you feel about it?

Andrew: I found it was very useful having the feedback because it usually meant she'd thought about it a bit, so it was clearer what she thought I could improve on, what was good, what was bad . . . And the last one, we had a short feedback session of about 15 mins and then she asked me to write one of those observation forms, she got me to write my own one, and she wrote one separately. Which was quite an interesting exercise, I quite enjoyed that . . . .

Interviewer: Did you feel your own concerns were invited and valued sufficiently?'

Andrew: Yes, I think they probably were. I can't ever recall having a problem with that because we just talked about the lesson and the class and she suggested things that I could improve on . . . and most of the time we were in agreement anyway. I am quite self-critical, self-analytical, so most of the things that she picked up I had already picked up on in other lessons anyway.

In this case, both the student and the observer were in general agreement but this is not always so. If the comments on the observation schedule have not really been agreed it is important that the student has a chance to offer his own perspective. This can be done formally, as in the following example:

Lesson 1: Student comment
It is an extravagant criticism to suggest that I neglected to follow lesson plans or set work that was too demanding. On one occasion I improvised on a lesson plan, because it was not working. I maintained the attention and interest of the class for most of the time and the class work has been encouraging. More professionalism in preparing worksheets and assessment in class is a priority of mine.

Lesson 2: Student comment
Owing to the nature of the questions set, some members of the class had problems distinguishing the length form the cross-section of a prism. This was not because the work was too advanced but because the focus of my exposition was inappropriate. The situation would have been helped had I taken the time to do the questions myself first.

Without the accompanying observation notes to compare, it is very difficult to interpret these comments but it does seem that the student is putting his finger on the very real difficulties he was having in adapting his plans mid-flow. Being criticised for doing this was hard to take when he was genuinely trying to respond to the pupils. In the second set of comments, the day after, his tone is more measured. Anyone reading these comments cannot fail to be struck by this student's honesty; he was clearly hurt and prepared to defend himself, but also able to accept responsibility for his omission after the second lesson.

REVIEWING PROGRESS

The opportunities and dilemmas in post-lesson observation feedback have been heightened by the previous examples. When it works well, both student and observer feel the benefit, but there are several pitfalls. Not least is the difficulty of timing. Straight after a lesson may not be the best time to talk, and several students ask for some time to reflect themselves before discussing the lesson. This is where the school-based mentor has the advantage, since she can include lesson observation discussion in the more general timetabled review sessions. It is important that a time and quiet place is set aside for these sessions, and that both the mentor and the student are prepared for them. Identifying a particular focus of concern, whether it is a particular class or a particular issue, e.g. planning, means that the time may be spent more productively. Having something specific to do as an outcome of the discussion is also desirable, and it is worth keeping written records of these sessions so that they can be referred to later, as in this brief summary written by the student himself:

> *Main focus:*
> Module and lesson planning
> Subject content
> Teaching methods
>
> *Agreed statement:*
> Good forward planning
> Inappropriate level of knowledge expected for one class
> Must see lesson plans as breakable guidelines
>
> *Forward planning:*
> Who sets the pace of the lessons – me, the children their work?

Reading between the lines here, we could conclude that the student is still working from his expectations of what the pupils should achieve, rather than responding to where they actually are. Although his final comment does not have a very specific strategy, it is clear that he is making an important shift in his thinking about practice. This could be the focus for the next lesson with this class, when the observer could look at how the student is seeking out and responding to the pupils, and how he is adapting his plans in action.

SELF-APPRAISAL

Throughout the year, the development of the students' self awareness and self evaluation is of prime importance. Many of the opportunities for such reflection are built in to the structure and practice of ITE courses, but there is always variation in the extent to which students will respond to this. Looking back and looking forward are, however, important habits to cultivate. Without marking progress, there will be little realisation of how much has been achieved; without looking forward and making considered plans, the young teacher may reach a safe but unexciting plateau.

Self-Appraisal 1 **End of diagnostic** **practice**	**Self-Appraisal 2** **Main practice** **Phase I**	**Self-Appraisal 3** **Main practice** **Phase 2**
Review I feel euphoric about the whole experience of teaching practice. I now am much more confident in myself, in my ability to structure my time through lesson planning, marking work, and actually teaching. As for strengths I was apprehensive about class management, but now feel that I coped very well in this field and varied my approach in different classes. A weakness I could pinpoint is perhaps making sure in the future that I inform my pupils of my marking criteria. I want to develop a working knowledge of examination structures as I am new to this system. I am happy at this point in subject application but want to delve further into differentiating work.	**Review** I don't feel as enthusiastic at the end of this term as I did on the diagnostic practice. My strengths in classroom management have become apparent as I have had to develop very quickly in this field. I am happier in my marking and assessment. I can maintain an orderly class, but not to the standard I am happy with. I would like some more experience of practical and investigational work as I am weak here.	**Review** I DID IT! I'm happier than I was at the end of the diagnostic practice. Had experience of 'A' level and was pleased to be observed successfully. I have really thought about and enjoyed my maths teaching. Teaching French was an excellent experience and I have been able to vary my approach and technique. My classroom management has greatly improved. I can control 7ALI!!! My IT delivery has been more organised and I have also done some coursework moderation. I could improve on long term planning.
Focus for improvement *(i) in the next phase of the course* Spend more time and thought on differentiation and assessment. Improve my knowledge of IT Improve my lesson timing (introduction, conclusion). *(ii) Before the end of the course* Use more applications in my teaching and provide contexts. Make sure I probe deeper into pupils' knowledge. Produce my own resources from computer.	**Focus for improvement** *(i) in the next phase* Work on coursework. *(ii) Before the end of the course* More work on IT.	**Focus for improvement** *(i) in the next phase* More professional work. More IT. Help with PSD, teaching. Work with high attainers. Work with low attainers.
Forward planning *(i) What help do you need?* More assistance with IT. Work with low and high attaining pupils. *(ii) What arrangements do you need to achieve this?* Attend another IT course. Ask school for sessions with above groups.	**Forward planning** *(i) What help do you need?* Experience of scheme of work preparation. Observation of more 'A' level classes. *(i) What arrangements do you need to achieve this?* Ask within dept.	**Forward planning** *(i) What help do you need?* Help from University and school on school based project (algebra in Year 8 for high attainers). Get information from new school on PSD curriculum. Look in library here before I leave. Ask about more reading on low attainers before I leave.

Figure 8.3 Self-appraisal statements

In the sequence of self-appraisal statements shown in Figure 8.3, it is clear that all has not been plain sailing, but it is also clear that the student has identified goals throughout the year and has achieved them. Many of these goals are in terms of new experiences, e.g. 'A' level work during the course, but the issues of attainment and differentiation are ongoing concerns, rather than goals, which many practising teachers continue to work at throughout their careers. In discussion with her tutor, this student was able to identify some useful reading (Ahmed, 1987; Haylock, 1991) which will help her think about working with low attainers, and there is still an extended project to do in school, which will help her to work more closely with a small group of high attainers in devising and evaluating curriculum materials. So the last weeks of the course can provide those students who have identified their needs with some final opportunities for further development.

FURTHER ON

The PGCE year is full of new experiences, and new situations. Trying to find out what students have actually learned depends largely on their ability to put this into words. When the student writes 'I have really thought about and enjoyed my maths teaching' what exactly does she mean? A multitude of possibilities rest behind this general statement.

When we read experienced teachers reflecting (Pratt, 1997) on their teaching, it is often very specific moments which they describe in detail which encapsulate their own self-knowledge. It is this move from the broad sweep to the very particular which may trigger self-evaluation of a deeply personal and productive nature.

REFERENCES

Ahmed, A. (1987) *Better Mathematics*. London: HMSO.
Haylock, D. (1991) *Teaching Mathematics to Low Attainers 8–12*. London: Paul Chapman,
Pratt, N. (1997) 'Shielding children from danger', *Mathematics Teaching*, **158**.

Part 3: Mathematics: Its Learning and Teaching

9: What is mathematics and what is it for?

There can hardly be a mathematics teacher who has not been asked by pupils 'Why are we doing this?' or 'What is the point of this?' in relation to some mathematics they have been teaching. Seeing these questions as genuine enquiries should stimulate teachers into questioning their own taken-for-granted assumptions and finding out more about the origin and development of the topic in question. This may enrich the teachers' own knowledge and help them to plan more meaningful lessons, but may also enable them to understand why pupils appear to be having major difficulties with particular concepts or skills. But looking at the mathematics on offer from the pupils' point of view also raises interesting issues about the relationship between school mathematics and mathematics in its widest sense.

MATHEMATICS ACROSS AND WITHIN CULTURES

Bishop (1988) identifies a core of common activities:

- counting
- locating (spatial acting, seeing and thinking)
- measuring
- designing
- playing and
- explaining

found across cultures and forming an empirical basis for mathematical thinking. He is talking about the similarities between practice in many different cultures around the world, but he (Bishop, 1991) also points out the particular role mathematics plays in the technologies of industrialised countries. These economically and politically dominant Western countries are able to shape a form of mathematics which is specialised, high status, and formally taught, unlike the common forms which arise more naturally in the everyday lives of people throughout the world. Let us look at some specific examples which shed light upon the relationship between these two forms of mathematics.

In and out of school in Brazil

The fascinating and painstaking research about the mathematics used by child street traders, carpenters, fishermen and construction workers in Brazil (Nunes *et al.*, 1993) is noteworthy for comparing performance in different situations. So the study of street children's performance compared their street and school mathematics practices, and the carpenters were contrasted with apprentices who were instructed in school. The study of uneducated fishermen investigated their understanding of proportionality, and the degree to which they could transfer their knowledge to unfamiliar situations.

Street traders

Five very poor street children, who had between one and eight years of schooling were studied performing informal calculations when selling goods on street corners or at markets. The researcher was in effect a customer, taping or writing down the children's responses and methods. Formal tests, based on the problems solved in the informal situation, were then devised and presented in the same place or at home. The questions involved either an arithmetic operation or a word problem and paper and pencil were available.

(1) First example (M, age 12)

Informal test
Customer: I'm going to take four coconuts. How much is that?
Child: There will be one hundred five, plus thirty, that's one thirty-five . . . one coconut is thirty-five . . . that is . . . one forty!

Formal test
Child solves the item 35 × 4, explaining out loud: 'Four times five is twenty, carry the two; two plus three is five, times four is twenty.' Answer written: 200.

(Nunes *et al.*, 1993: 24)

This was a typical example where the same mathematical problem was performed correctly in the informal situation and incorrectly in the formal situation. In fact 98.2% of the responses overall were correct in the street situation and 73.7% in the formal situation, with only 36.8 % of the arithmetical operations responses correct. This difference in success rate in itself is noteworthy but the fact that the children had entirely different methods for questions which had essentially the same mathematical structure is also of great significance. When working informally, the children were using mental methods and communicating their results orally, and the methods used were closely tied to the actual numbers involved. When working formally, the methods were school taught methods, often used inaccurately, with multiplication and addition confused. Once committed to working on paper the children seemed to lose a feel for the reasonableness of the answer.

Mathematics in fishing communities

One of the arguments in favour of the compressed algorithmic methods often taught in schools is that they are generalisable – they will work whatever the numbers used or across different contexts. It is often thought that informal methods lack this versatility, and may tie the user to particular situations. Another part of the Brazilian study, not as widely known as the work with the street children but just as illuminating, looked at these issues in depth by researching fishermen's use and understanding of proportionality.

These fishermen would sell their catch to middlemen, who then processed it in some way, i.e. by salting and drying fish, or shelling crab or shrimps. The researchers used this feature of the context to explore the fishermen's ability to solve proportionality problems of increasing difficulty and also where the context was similar but unfamiliar, i.e. questions about cassava, an agricultural product which is ground, squeezed and dried before being sold as a kind of flour.

The fishermen had very little schooling and only 2 out of the 22 had reached the grade at which they would have encountered proportionality. It is clear that the fishermen did demonstrate an understanding of proportionality beyond the simplest case, and within the harder type questions there was even some success when the desired number was neither a multiple or divisor of the number given:

> 18 kilos of unprocessed seafood yields 3 kilos of processed food.
> How much would be needed for a customer who wants 2 kilos?

> After having attempted the problem once and failing, J.A.S. returned to it and gave the correct answer . . .

> J.A.S.:   one and a half kilos [processed] would be nine [unprocessed], it has to be nine, because half of eighteen is nine and half of three is one and a half. And a half kilo[processed] is three kilos [unprocessed]. Then it'd be nine plus three is twelve [unprocessed]; the twelve kilos would give two kilos [processed].

> (Nunes *et al.*, 1993: 112)

The fishermen also revealed that they could transfer across contexts because in the later questions about beans and cassava, success rates were similar to those in the fishing contexts.

These examples clearly show that the concept of proportionality does not have to be taught, that the fisherman could go beyond the simple calculations they used every day and were able to transfer their knowledge. Everyday practices for them, then, were generalisable to a degree. In other studies – which compared farmers, construction workers and carpenters with students who had more years of schooling – the students were no more successful than the workers and they sometimes gave ridiculous answers in the contexts of the problems e.g. walls of length 330 mm or 33 cm.

Maths at Work in the West

In 1985, the Maths at Work project based at the University of Bath set out to produce and trial a set of curriculum materials based on case studies of young people using mathematics in a variety of jobs. Common skills were identified and examples created which could be used to illustrate the relevance of mathematics. Even at the time the authors noted that the employment opportunities for the target group, school leavers of 16, were deteriorating. They were also aware that the materials on their own would be unable to convey the reality of the workplace and that: 'There are occasions where rules of thumb have evolved at work which might offend the finer feelings of mathematicians. ' (Austwick, *et al.*, 1985: vi)

The case studies make fascinating reading, with a wide variety of jobs, e.g. laboratory assistant, apprentice bookbinder, fisheries inspector; and using groups of skills, e.g. calculations related to measurement, statistical methods, percentages and cost related problems, drawings and related calculations.

It is very clear that many of the jobs required the repeated use of the same standard procedures and that pre-set tables and routines could be learned with practice. So for example, neither the derivation or rearrangement of a formula appeared but the substitution of values into a standard formula appeared in several cases. Of course, many of these jobs will have altered within the last ten years with increased automation and the greater use of information technology, except in small firms where the equipment is not cost effective. Skills which are still relevant today are less concerned with routine calculations and more with, say, estimation, approximation, spatial awareness, and the judgement of quantities. It was interesting to see such skills being highlighted in the materials.

(a) John: cutting room ancillary at an overalls factory

Example 1
He needed to lay out ten lengths of cloth each 4.5 m long, so he needed 45 m of cloth. In the warehouse there were three rolls, one with 40 m left, one with 140 m left, and one with 9 m left. He has several choices but decides to take two lengths from the nine metre roll and the rest from the 40 m roll, to avoid leaving a small piece at the end of a roll.
Is he correct?

Example 2
He needs to lay out the pattern pieces for the overalls so that there is very little waste material. Head Office want an 85% utilisation figure based on the formula:

$$\% \text{ utilisation } = \frac{\text{area of pattern}}{\text{area of cloth}} \times 100$$

His first layout gives about 60% so he has to adjust the pattern pieces and try again until he comes closer to 85%.

(b) Helen: design apprentice with a company which manufactures wrappers

Existing wrappers were 8" by 10", and they need to make bigger ones the same shape but 11" long.

Helen knew that she had to use the two numbers, 10 and 11 to make a fraction. She also knew that she had to increase the length. So she made a fraction with the bigger number on top.

Comparisons

In both the Brazilian and British situations, the mathematics was subsumed within purposeful activities with defined goals. Formality, in the shape of taught algorithms, was problematic for the street children, and applying their formal knowledge was problematic for the school students when compared with the carpenters. In the case of the British school leavers, straightforward general methods were already provided and were learned with repeated practice, although judgement and the refinement of strategies was also needed in some situations. Of course, someone else derived and presented those methods to the school leavers, so there was clearly a need for someone else to have acquired the sort of mathematical understanding which would enable them to provide these algorithmic methods.

All this research points to an uneasy relationship between the formal mathematics taught in schools and the mathematics which people do as part of their problem-solving activity out of school. Improving this relationship is an important task. In teaching, Bishop warns against decontextualising ideas too rapidly and argues against a fixed body of esoteric knowledge belonging to a privileged few, so that school mathematics builds upon the learner's own culturally familiar activities. So in the case of the street children, the street methods could have been used as a starting point for work on number operations in school instead of presenting the children with completely unrelated methods.

This argument is relevant in the mathematics classrooms of England and Wales. Presenting pupils with contextual or practical activities is clearly desirable but we also want to provide pupils with an understanding of underlying principles and concepts, so that they can make a bridge to the formality and abstraction which gives much of school mathematics its generalisability and power. We know, however, that this move is fraught with difficulty (Johnson, 1989). One possible way out of the difficulty is to provide the vast majority of our pupils with only the mathematics which will be of immediate use to them in their everyday lives, and to reserve the abstract mathematics for those pupils who can handle this transition easily.

Separating pupils in this way has not been successful in the past. Both sets of pupils were given a restricted diet – with one concentrating excessively on utilitarian aspects, and the other group focusing on abstract theory remote from applications. Teachers should remember the notion of entitlement which is embedded within the National Curriculum – that all pupils should have a variety of mathematical experiences within the defined areas, with real-life applications as well as pure mathematical reasoning. It is for them to find ways of teaching which build up from pupils' own personal experiences but extend their horizons, whatever their background or attainment level. And if we look at Bishop's list again, we can certainly identify links between it and the sections in the National Curriculum:

- *Counting*   Ma2 (number)
- *Location*   Ma3 (shape, space and measures)
- *Measuring*   Ma3 (shape, space and measures)
- *Designing*   Ma1, Ma3 (making decisions to solve problems, shape, space and measures)
- *Playing*   Ma4 (probability) Ma1(investigating within mathematics itself)
- *Explaining*   Ma1 (the communications strand and the reasoning strand) Ma4 (handling data)

Broad areas which seem to be missing are algebra and proof. In algebra we are looking at generality – relationships which are abstracted from the particular features of a situation, and which can be expressed in a form of language or symbolism, with its own particular rules and conventions. Working confidently with this symbolism is akin to using a second language fluently. Algebraic symbolism is vital in modelling and is a crucial tool in advanced technology, but it also opens up to us new possibilities in pure mathematics. For some people, proof is what distinguishes mathematics from the other sciences, giving it its logical, deductive character. These two features, together with an emphasis on conceptual understanding rather than problem solving, are highly valued in formally taught mathematics curricula and distinguish it from the mathematical activities common to all humankind. Providing a bridge between 'common' mathematical knowledge and the more mysterious world of symbols and philosophy should be an important priority.

HISTORICAL INSIGHTS

School mathematics is often presented with little reference to its development over time or to the people who have shaped this process. For instance, the development of the number system is a fascinating study in its own right, but the story offers more than mathematical insights – we may also understand how, for instance, children may find the ideas of fractions more difficult than we anticipate or that accepting a rule like 'two minuses make a plus' at face value may indicate a worrying lack of intellectual curiosity.

Fractions

The difficulties which pupils have with fractions have been well documented (Dickson *et al.*, 1984) but when we look at the development of the concept and notation throughout history this should come as less of a surprise. Rather than blaming teachers for poor teaching we come to realise that here we have some mathematics which is intrinsically quite difficult and complex. From interpretations of a 1650 BC copy of the original Rhind papyrus we can surmise that the Egyptians (Gardiner, 1957) had a very specific meaning and notation for fractions which does not correspond neatly with our modern practice. So

would mean the fifth part of a row of five equal parts . There would only be one fifth, the last part in the row. It just would not have made sense to the Egyptians to divide up the whole into five equal parts and to say that each was a fifth; still less would they group several fifths together and create non-unitary fractions, like three fifths. The only two exceptions to this were the use of two thirds and the very rare three quarters which may have had slightly different meanings as the complementary parts left over when the third and the fourth part had been removed. With this conception of fractions the Egyptians were left with the awkward job of expressing complex fractions as the sum of unitary fractions,

$$\text{e.g. our } \frac{4}{7} \text{ by } \frac{1}{2} + \frac{1}{14}$$

which to us seems amazingly cumbersome and clever at the same time.

Expressing fractions in terms of the denominator 60 came down from the Babylonians and was still in use in the sixteenth century, whereas the denominator of 12 originated with the Romans. In Imperial measures, expressing someone's height as 5' 7" is really a form of fractional notation, as is the angular measure 30° 23' 45" (thirty degrees, twenty three minutes and forty five seconds). Naturally, when these standard denominators are used, many of the problems which school children have traditionally had with adding fractions disappear, and it is easy to see why decimal fractions have been so successful a development in the context of measurement and money. Even so the decimal notation we now take for granted has been a long time settling down, since an early form was introduced in the sixteenth century by the Dutch engineer, Simon Stevin.

It would be foolish to suggest that the move to decimal notation in much of our everyday life has made number work easier for pupils. They do not have to grapple with tedious fractional sums so much but they do need a sophisticated grasp of the base ten place value system. Some argue compellingly for abandoning the teaching of fractions altogether. Writing from North America, Groff (1992) questions the usefulness of fractions, their place in genuine problems, and their role as a prerequisite for algebraic study, considering them to be a pedagogical anachronism. His arguments against wasting pupils' time in developing the *skills* of operating on fractions are persuasive, although there may still be a place for some fractions work in *supporting conceptual understanding* of the place value system and in giving pupils some knowledge of the history of mathematics. Where Groff makes an interesting departure from conventional critiques of curricular content is in advocating the role of teachers in determining how much should be taught:

> At present, teachers are directed to teach fractions (often against their better judgements, they informally tell me), or else risk the ignominy of having their professional reputations adversely affected. Teachers . . . must become the impartial jury for determining the fate of fractions instruction.

Whether teachers are confident enough to take this responsibility, of course, owes much to their feelings of autonomy and the political climate in which they are working. Some are much happier to deliver a curriculum constructed by someone else and to follow a line of progression which is denied by the reality of their experiences in the classroom. In the case of fractions, they still have a place in the NC but it is good to see that references at the lower levels are in the context of sensible practical activities, and are linked with work on decimals and percentages, whereas operations on fractions do not appear until level 8. Just thinking about the reasoning behind the standard rules for adding, subtracting, multiplying and dividing fractions should cause any PGCE student to blanch. It is an exercise well worth trying, along with finding sensible contexts for such operations.

Directed numbers

The discussion about fractions centred largely upon their perceived usefulness in practical situations:

> *Herodotus (mid-fifth century BC)*
> The king moreover (so they say) divided the country amongst all the Egyptians by giving each an equal yearly square parcel of land, and made this his source of revenue, appointing the payment of a yearly tax. And any man who was robbed by the river of a part of his land would come to Sesostris and declare what had befallen him; then the king would send men to look into it and measure the space by which the land was diminished, so that thereafter it should pay in proportion to the tax originally proposed.
>
> (Fauvel and Grey, 1987: 21)

Other extensions to the number system, however, were constructed as solutions to dilemmas arising out of pure mathematical situations remote from directly practical situations, and widespread applications appeared much later. The first example of an isolated negative number appeared in the fifteenth century in an equation in Chuquet's *Triparty*, but because he wrote in French and his works were only in manuscript many of his ideas did not have a great influence. Cardano, in the next century, had a much wider circulation with his *Ars magna*, a comprehensive work on algebra containing rules for solving different types of cubic equations, usually expressed in geometric terms and solved in ways unfamiliar to many of us:

Demonstration

For example, let the cube of GH and six times the side GH be equal to 20. I take two cubes AE and Cl whose difference shall be 20 . . . .

Rule

Cube the third part of the number of 'things', to which you add the square of half the number of the equation, and take the root of the whole, that is, the square root, which you will use, in the one case, subtracting the same half, and you will have a 'binomial' and 'apotome' respectively . . . .

(Cardano, translated by R.B. McLennon, in Fauvel and Grey, 1987: 261–2)

In other solutions Cardano accepted negative answers although he described such roots as 'fictitious' and he also worked with the square roots of negative numbers, thus anticipating the creation of complex numbers.

This excursion not only demonstrates how mathematics has grown in response to problems within mathematics itself, but it also shows how ideas took time to develop and become accepted. Moreover, we see how algebraic symbolism has developed and how in the process, problems which were stated geometrically, now adopt a life of their own. Whereas Cardano was unwilling to go beyond the powers of one (a line) two (a square) and three (a cube) our algebraic symbolism allows us to play with any powers we like, without recourse to geometrical representation and this in turn leads on to new branches of often completely abstract mathematics.

The history of the extension of the number system shows us that new kinds of numbers were accepted because they became useful both in pure mathematics and in practical situations or in science, but in fact the foundational basis of arithmetic was not shored up until well after fractions, directed numbers and complex numbers were all well known – in the second half of the nineteenth century. This is particularly interesting since it contrasts with much school mathematics where tidy definitions and rules are often taught before pupils attempt to explore or use the ideas in question. Is there something we can learn here?

On the one hand, the realisation that some ideas have taken a long time to develop may encourage us to be more patient with pupils who are finding difficulty. So we may let big ideas take longer to grow in a child's mind and continue to revisit and explore them. We may be much more circumspect about imposing definitions and work together with pupils in refining definitions of concepts which grow out of reflecting on problems after they have been solved. On the other, we could say that breakthroughs in technique or symbolism enable us to teach more earlier, and that we have a debt to previous mathematicians in making our work as teachers much easier. All we have to do is bring our pupils up to date with everything there is to know about mathematics, at which point they will be in a position to go out and create some more. The trouble with this argument is that to be brought up to date, pupils may have learned to be passive receivers of old knowledge and may not have developed the ability to ask questions, criticise the taken for granted or found out ways of coping with being stuck. We may be teaching mathematics without creating people who can think mathematically.

SHAPING MATHEMATICS AND SHAPING THE MATHEMATICS CURRICULUM

Mathematics, and indeed mathematics teaching, has always been strongly influenced by the social and political context in which it has been studied. For instance, in the early part of the nineteenth century, mathematics in France and Germany had totally different emphases. For a short time, utilitarianism was paramount to French mathematicians whereas in Germany pure mathematics was valued more highly.

After the revolution the French educational system totally collapsed, and the setting up of the short-lived *Ecole Normale* and later the *Ecole Polytechnique* illustrate a profound shift in mathematical activity. From being the preserve of an intellectual élite, mathematics now became a more democratic activity. The *Ecole Normale* was set up to train teachers so that they could disseminate mathematical knowledge throughout the country, with Paris as the centre of the system. The leading mathematicians of the country gave lectures, some of which were printed for wider consumption

Subsequently, the systematic training of students in mathematics, science and engineering at the *Ecole Polytechnique* led on to their more specialised training in the School of Bridges and Roads, the School of Mining, the School of Artillery and other technical institutions. Gaspard Monge was a leading figure in French educational reorganisation, and although he later fell out of favour when the Bourbon monarchy was restored, his ideas for raising the level of teaching were lastingly influential. One of these was the writing of textbooks, so that advanced knowledge was made more uniform but also so that students could be prepared for the highly competitive entrance examinations for the *Ecole Polytechnique*. Mathematics itself at that time was viewed as an extremely important subject for study, dominating teaching throughout the country. It was also seen as a contrast to religious authority, based on clear and rigorous reasoning. This fitted well with the philosophy of the atheists who wanted to undermine the authority of the Church and appeal to people's reason, not their religious obedience. It is interesting that central control, uniformity, assessment and the moral and spiritual dimension of the curriculum feature today in our National Curriculum. *Plus ca change*!

If looking at history can give us insights into teaching, looking at the gaps in history can be just as illuminating. It becomes clear that in recorded history we rarely hear the voices of the powerless or the marginalised. Just as mathematicians writing in their vernacular found acceptance harder to obtain than those writing in the more prestigious Latin, so the child in the classroom who explains mathematics in his or her own words may find it more difficult to have their ideas valued. The contribution of the poor and uneducated to the development of any high status knowledge is explicable in terms of lack of access and opportunity, but perhaps the most obvious gap in mathematics is that of the contribution of women, even from those of the privileged social orders.

Even today, the explanations for this absence hinge upon biological determinism arguments and social conditioning arguments. When De Morgan, who was a supporter of the work of Ada, Countess of Lovelace, said of mathematics that 'the very great tension of mind which [women] require is beyond the strength of a woman's physical power of application' (Stein, 1985) he was referring to biological limitations. Later writers have referred to brain structure, not endurance, to explore spatial abilities but the research here is inconclusive, because it is so difficult to separate latent abilities from the kinds of spatial activity which males and females traditionally experience. For instance, the Assessment of Performance Unit (1988) found that differences on spatial items evened out when curricular choices were controlled. Work on social conditioning is similarly complex, because there are so many hidden and competing variables at play here, e.g. teacher expectations, classroom dynamics, parents, single-sex or mixed-sex teaching, but it is in this area that intervention strategies have been adopted in schools.

What is clear, however, is that the traditional picture of underachievement and low participation in higher mathematics is not stable across different countries (Hanna, 1989) and that it is changing. Moreover, the traditional focus has been questioned, posing as it does a deficit view of girls, and there is more interest now in why high-achieving girls make a positive choice away from mathematics. We also need to recognise that the differences between high-achieving and low-achieving pupils of whatever sex are much greater than differences between the sexes.

An intriguing question remains. If mathematics is a human product, and so many professional mathematicians are male, then would different sorts of academic mathematics be created or different aspects be emphasised if more women were represented?

Technological advances in society also impinge upon mathematics, and this is seldom a straightforward process. Consider the way in which calculators have been incorporated into the curriculum. Despite carefully reasoned arguments and official though guarded sanction, calculators are still being used to solve the sorts of problem which existed before they became commonplace, instead of being used to handle larger quantities of real data which would be cumbersome to process without technology. Both these cases point to the difficulty of changing educational practice, and the importance of recognising the complexity of such change:

> The school curriculum, however, is a conservative social institution. In this context, decisive change, even though based on logical argument and research evidence, is likely to be resisted. Some aspects of school activity are treasured as fundamental: and proposals which appear to devalue these aspects encounter a backlash of personal and political prejudice and something called 'common sense'. If there is something to be learned from the history of calculators in school, it is that research which identifies educational benefits is not sufficient to promote curriculum development. We also need a greater understanding of the mechanisms through which development can take place and become acceptable.
>
> (Costello, 1992: 23)

Costello puts his finger on the view of the curriculum as a site of struggle. The whole notion of the curriculum as a *selection* of material is highlighted and this may help teachers to see a personal role in being involved in this process. Opportunities are available at school level in the choice of, say, coursework activities, at a local level in being involved with an examination board in drawing up new syllabuses and at a national level in responding to invitations to consultation over curriculum policy.

A recent example of this was when the 1994 draft proposals for the revised Mathematics National Curriculum went out to consultation, resulting in the retention of 'Using and applying mathematics' as a separate component in the new curriculum. Whichever way the respondents felt about this, here was an opportunity to argue a case with colleagues and to put forward a view which could shape the way in which the future mathematics curriculum would be structured. It was an important argument about the nature of mathematics, and although that argument continues to be worked out in practice in classrooms, what is written in the policy document clearly has an influence.

One of the key messages which comes across from the present structure is that

- using mathematics
- communicating mathematics, and
- reasoning and proof

are all mathematics, and it is no accident that verbs feature prominently here. That mathematics is seen as a purposeful activity which people do rather than a collection of facts and techniques to be copied is not a new perspective, but one which is frequently denied in the reality of classroom practice. This phenomenon has been noted with monotonous regularity and was memorably described in the Cockcroft report:

> Mathematics lessons in secondary schools are very often not about anything. You collect like terms, or learn the laws of indices, with no perception of why anyone needs to do such things. There is excessive preoccupation with a sequence of skills and quite inadequate opportunity to see the skills emerging from the solution to problems.

> (Cockcroft, 1982, para. 462)

The wonder of this is that lessons which are 'not about anything' are still taking place in classrooms up and down the land at this very moment. At the heart of this problem are some difficult tensions. Pupils need to have some mathematical content knowledge if they are going to solve problems, or prove results, but if we fill them with content knowledge only they will either switch off or never develop the strategies needed to use and apply what they know. This relationship between problem solving, conceptual understanding and mathematical skills is with us again.

THE PURPOSES OF THE MATHEMATICS CURRICULUM

In our sophisticated industrial society, the curriculum serves many purposes and mathematics is valued for a variety of reasons, e.g.:

- it can be useful at a very basic level in most people's everyday life
- it is useful in some jobs and central in others
- it is useful in other academic disciplines
- it can act as a filter for selecting applicants for a particular career or course
- it is a means of understanding and communicating quantitative information
- it is part of our history
- it is a way of thinking, and of exploring ideas which may not have any immediate application.

This is my own arbitrary list, with no particular priority implied in the order although there is a general move from utility to more intellectual aspects. These different dimensions were all strongly supported in the original proposals for the mathematics national curriculum:

> ... the power of mathematics in tackling practical problems from everyday life and the world of work justifies its position in the school curriculum ... [but] mathematics is not only taught because it is useful. It should also be a source of delight and wonder, offering pupils intellectual excitement, for example in the discovery of relationships, the pursuit of rigour and the achievement of elegant solutions ...
>
> (DfE, 1988: 3,4)

and it was recognised that mathematics has an important role to play in preparing pupils not only for the world of work, but for active citizenship and responsibilities as members of households.

The working group gave examples of the mathematics used in a range of jobs and at every level of employment (Table 9.1) and examples of its pervasiveness across the school curriculum were also given (Table 9.2).

Besides this, however, it was felt that mathematics contributed towards developing the general skills of communication, reasoning, and problem-solving and qualities such as 'perseverance; imagination and flexibility; self management and team working skills; and perhaps above all, a "can do" attitude to life's challenges.'

At that time, the intention was to include these personal qualities alongside the ability to apply and communicate mathematics within the assessment structure, but this idea was never accepted. Such intentions can of course be realised by teachers who recognise that such personal skills may be carried into all areas of their pupils' adult lives, long after examination success or failure has been forgotten. Of course, the public assessment system has always exerted an influence upon the curriculum and this is becoming stronger as the fear of industrial decline has fuelled the drive for higher standards. But it is seriously worrying that pupils may leave school associating mathematics with either examination success or failure, without appreciating

Table 9.1 Mathematics for employment

Arithmetic (young school leavers)	
Commonly needed	calculations with one or more operation
	proportion
	percentages
	substitution in formulae (money & other quantities)
	recall of number bonds
	recall of multiplication tables
	calculator use for numerous calculations
	decimals, metric system
	interpretation of numerical and graphical data from computers
Rare	long written processes
	written calculations with fractions
Algebraic manipulation (higher technical levels)	engineering and construction industries
Geometry and trigonometry	engineering and building industries
	preparation of drawings and practical work
Computer use	weather and economic forecasting
	aerodynamical and structural design
Statistics and data handling	quality control and assurance
	management information
Logic	software engineering

Table 9.2 Mathematics across the school curriculum

data handling	history, biology
measurement (ratio, scale)	art, technology, science, geography
algebra	science

its contribution towards their personal development or its pervasiveness in our social and cultural lives. Nowhere is this more obvious than in the newspapers.

Being able to understand and evaluate information like this puts all of us in a position to make choices and take control of aspects of our lives. Being able to do this is surely far more important than being able to do, say, a long multiplication sum without a calculator and yet has received far less media attention. On the one hand, mathematical illiteracy is a form of damaging ignorance:

> Even more ominous is the gap between scientists' assessments of various risks and the popular perceptions of those risks, a gap that threatens eventually to lead either to unfounded and crippling anxieties or to impossible and economically paralysing demands for risk-free guarantees. Politicians are seldom a help in this regard since they deal with public opinion and are therefore loath to clarify the likely hazards and trade-offs associated with almost any policy.
>
> (Paulos, 1990)

On the other, lacking an appreciation of the beauty or puzzlement in mathematics is as sad as being shut off from music, art or literature. Ian Stewart has done much to demystify mathematics and increase the public's understanding and appreciation of it. In this newspaper article, he is describing how the scientist, Benoit Mandelbrot, recognised a common thread running throughout his work and in so doing stimulated a new branch of geometry:

> Mandelbrot decided that his kind of structure needed a name and he invented one: 'fractal'. A fractal is a geometric shape, such as a graph of stockmarket prices, that has fine structure on all scales of magnification. Most familiar forms in the natural world are fractals – a tree, for example, has structure on many scales: trunk, bough, limb, branch, twig. So does a bush, a fern, or a cauliflower. A lump of rock looks like an entire mountain in miniature; a small cloud looks just as complicated as a big one if you view it close up . . . .
>
> They are all fractals. The traditional shapes of mathematics do not behave like this. If you magnify a sphere, then its surface becomes flatter and flatter, resembling a featureless plane. Mathematicians began to understand how much their subject could be expanded by embracing Mandelbrot's geometry.
>
> (Stewart, 1996)

The twist in the tail of this story is that besides being fascinating, the study of fractals led to developments in the way in which images are produced on computer screens. So we have moved from utility via communication to beauty and back to utility again.

CONCLUSIONS: THE NATURES OF MATHEMATICS

If anything, the theme which emerges from this chapter is that of mathematics as a human activity, with all the richness and diversity which that implies. On the one hand, mathematics is pervasive across cultures and time, and on the other it is highly specialised and even obscure. Mathematics exists in the world of ideas and in the mud of the construction site. We can expand mathematical systems such as the number system without any idea that the new constructions may turn out to be useful, or we can devise new methods and techniques in direct response to practical problems. Knowledge in mathematics involves understanding meanings and relationships, say, between functions and their derivatives, or between fractions, decimals and percentages and also knowing when to use this understanding, but it can equally well refer to the ability to formulate a solution to a problem where the approach is not obvious and there may be some false trails.

So what answers would I give to those questioning pupils at the beginning of the chapter? With the benefit of experience, reading, reflection and discussion over a period of years I am better prepared for these questions than when I was a young teacher. Better still, I am now ready to provide a justification before the question is even asked as I now have a better developed sense of purpose than before. These are just some of my own aims which have governed both what and how I have taught in a variety of situations in the past:

- I want you to puzzle this out for yourselves.
- You will probably need this fact/ skill/ way of thinking at this point.
- So that you gain a greater personal understanding through sharing with others.
- Because this is a very useful thing to know.
- This is a really powerful idea and it took human beings a long time to develop it.
- I want to share my own fascination with you.
- This is very attractive and pleasing.
- You will need this for your next assignment, exercise, examination . . .
- I do not know how to solve this myself.
- You need to prove that your idea will always work.
- You need to practise and revise what we have been doing, so that you consolidate your understanding.
- You will all learn more if you work together.

When you can share your intentions with pupils in this way, it is usually much easier to teach. The pupils have a clearer idea of the agenda, and will know what to expect and what not to expect. Moreover, if you are offering them a variety of opportunities over time they will begin to see how the jigsaw can fit together, and have a better idea of the different experiences which go together to make a balanced mathematical diet. This sharing of values and purposes does not have to stop at the classroom door, of course. It is food for discussion with colleagues, with parents and with the many adults who still wonder what mathematics is all about well after they have left school.

REFERENCES

Assessment of Performance Unit (1988) *Attitudes and Gender Differences*. Berkshire: NFER-Nelson.

Austwick, K., Richards, P.N. and Livingston, K.M. (1985) *Maths at Work, Teacher's Guide*. Cambridge: Cambridge University Press.

Bishop, A.J. (1988) *Mathematical Enculturation*. Dordrecht: Kluwer.

Bishop, A.J. (1991) 'Mathematical values in the teaching process,' in *Mathematical Knowledge: its Growth Through Teaching*, A.J. Bishop, S. Mellin-Olsen and J. Van Dormolen (eds). London: Kluwer.

Cockcroft, W.H. (Chair) (1982) *Mathematics Counts, Report of the Committee of Inquiry into the Teaching of Mathematics in Schools*. London: HMSO.

Costello, J. (1992) 'A Failed Revolution', *Micromath*, 8(1).

Department for Education (1988) *Mathematics for Ages 5 to 16: Proposals for the Secretary of State for Education and Science and the Secretary of State for Wales*. London: HMSO.

Dickson, L., Brown, M., and Gibson, O. (1984) *Children Learning Mathematics*. London: Cassell.

Fauvel, J. and Grey, J. (1987) *The History of Mathematics*. Basingstoke: Macmillan Press in association with the Open University.

Gardiner, A. (1957) *Egyptian Grammar*. Oxford: Oxford University Press.

Groff, P (1992) 'A future for fractions?', *Mathematics Teaching*, **140**.

Haggerty, L. (1995) *New ideas for Teacher Education, A Mathematics Framework*. London: Cassell.

Hanna, G. (1989) 'Mathematics Achievement of girls and boys in grade eight: Results from twenty countries', in *Educational Studies in Mathematics*, **20**, 225–32.

Johnson, D. (ed.) (1989) *Children's Mathematical Frameworks 81–3*. Berkshire: NFER-Nelson.

Nunes, T., Schliemann, A. Dias, and Carraher, D.W. (1993) *Street Mathematics and School Mathematics*. Cambridge: Cambridge University Press.

Paulos, J.A. (1990) *Innumeracy: Mathematical Illiteracy and its Consequence.*, London: Penguin.

Smith, R. (1996) 'Something for the grown ups', in *The Role of Higher Education in Initial Teacher Education*, J. Furlong and R. Smith (eds). London: Kogan Page.

Stein, D. (1985) *Ada; a Life and a Legacy*. MIT press.

Stewart, I. (1996) 'A fractal paints a thousand works', *The Sunday Times, Science section*, **8 September**, 10.9.

10: Learning and teaching mathematics

Having looked at the complexity of mathematics, what are the implications for student teachers? We have seen that mathematics is an activity carried out across cultures and throughout time, and that school mathematics has its own particular, and fairly recent, place in the scheme of things. The assumption is that by setting up compulsory education and creating the roles of teacher and pupil we can ensure learning, but this is by no means straightforward. Griffin (1989) examines this dilemma by using John Mason's words: 'Teaching takes place in time, learning takes place over time'.

This tension is clearly identified by students throughout their training, as they build up considerable tacit knowledge of pupils learning and failing to learn mathematics, and of the complexity of the teaching act. Simple mechanistic ideas of learning are soon replaced by the acknowledgement of many different factors which affect learning and which may be loosely categorised as:

1.   Contextual and social factors – the effect of situations and other people.
2.   Affective factors – feelings, beliefs and expectations.
3.   Cognitive factors – what is going on in the mind.

As learners themselves, student teachers will realise how these factors overlap and the difficulty of concentrating on any one group of factors in isolation. Without some sort of structure, however, it is impossible to grapple with this complex topic so in the following sections, extracts of data from PGCE students and some examples of research will be used to illuminate these different aspects of learning, and show how they can interact within a teaching situation. The final section will pull together these aspects and consider contemporary theories of learning and their possible implications for teaching.

CONTEXTUAL AND SOCIAL FACTORS

The organisation of classes

The value and autonomy of the individual are strong principles underlying much of Western social policy and practice, not least in education. Teachers are obliged to treat pupils as individuals with their own abilities, backgrounds, attitudes and difficulties (NCC, 1992: 15) and very few would claim to do otherwise. In mathematics teaching, the importance of recognising the different constructions which pupils may bring is similarly stressed:

1. No learner can be expected to think in the same way as his or her teacher.
2. No two learners in a class can be expected to think in the same way as each other (possibly excepting twins).

(Backhouse *et al.*, 1992: 54)

If there is so much individual variation in the way students think about mathematics, then it is clearly going to be very difficult for teachers to cater adequately for a truly mixed attainment group unless they are provided with individual programmes. This is the intention behind individualised learning schemes such as SMILE, KENT and, to a lesser extent, SMP. Here, pupils work at their own pace through commercially produced materials with periodic tests and reviews to assess their progress.

Such schemes are carefully designed and trialed, with consistent approaches to concepts and topics and a variety of opportunities including games and practical work. This takes away the burden of task preparation, but imposes an increased administrative role upon the teacher, which can be difficult for the student teacher to learn when the materials are unfamiliar. It is also difficult to keep an eye on everyone and to ensure that all the pupils are working, since the teacher can fall into the trap of only reacting to the pupils who ask for help. Another disadvantage is that pupils encounter their mathematics in a pre-determined way, largely by reading the text of the cards or booklets, but in many of the schools which use them there are also lessons 'away from the scheme' in which different learning experiences are offered. With an individualised scheme, the potentially damaging effects of labelling pupils by setting can be avoided since everyone is working at their own pace, with high attainers working alongside low attainers in the same classroom.

Despite this possibility with its emphasis upon the individual, setting is very common in secondary mathematics classes and is usually done earlier than in most other subjects.

The intention behind setting is to produce homogeneous attainment groups which can be taught as a whole class. This often entails the class being taught as if it were an individual. Everyone receives the same explanations and worked examples, is expected to follow the sequence which is in the teacher's head, and is expected to master the material at approximately the same rate. Paradoxically, though, the expectation of homogeneity may encourage the teacher to have an 'ideal' individual for whom the material is targeted, and the inevitable differences within the group may appear more dramatic than if a variety of responses were expected.

Trying to have successful individual programmes for each pupil has disadvantages, and yet treating the class as a completely homogeneous group is not ideal either. The real challenge is to cater for individuals within a group, and to cater for the group through its individuals, not as if it were an individual.

This was illustrated by a student teacher interviewed at the end of his course, when he suggested that a variety of methods can be shared with pupils:

> '. . . the first one was on er when it was on rearranging algebraic expressions . . . a fun subject with the Year 9's. And er just the way we were trying different approaches, we were trying different approaches to cover this because it's kind of

a hit and miss thing, because some processes kids will easily pick up on, some kids easily pick up on, and then other processes other kids . . . and they all do the same thing, so we had to go through a few until they'd found one that they wanted. Then there is positive and negative aspects of that because by doing a few they think maybe they have to do all of them, they don't realise that they can pick one of them, the positive thing is that by the time you have done three or four then most of them will have found one that they can do.'

It is not clear from this student's account if he provided the different methods or if they arose from the pupils themselves, but it does seem as if he has found a way to use different ways of thinking about the same problem to further the learning in the whole group. In this case, the class was setted but the student had not assumed that the pupils would all be clones of one another.

Different forms of setting are found in different schools. Some primary schools are now using setting for their Key Stage 2 pupils, especially in preparation for the tiered NC test papers, but in the secondary school, setting during or at the end of the pupils' first year is very common.

Given that setting is such a common feature of mathematics departments, Askew and Wiliam (1995: 40) were surprised that there has been so little research in this area in this country, so their guarded conclusions that: 'mathematical attainment group-ings can lead to some gains in attainment' and that 'Contrary to popular belief, setting does not appear to lead necessarily to low self esteem for low attainers' is based largely on research from the USA. Clearly more work needs to be done here, but there appear to be some grounds for accepting that setting by attainment is not necessarily damaging.

All my encounters with students and teachers reinforce the evidence (Ruthven, 1987; Watson, 1996) that ability is used by teachers of mathematics, more than any other subject, as a major organising principle for their teaching. This view of ability as the main contributory factor in achievement (Lorenz, 1982), that it is stable and persistent over time, with little variation allowed for particular tasks or in different situations (MacIntyre and Brown, 1978) could amount to a self-fulfilling prophecy which does not say much for mathematics teachers' confidence in their ability to make a difference. Again a short excerpt shows student teachers grappling with these uncomfortable insights:

S1:   Isn't that what Cockcroft was going on about . . . it was him wasn't it . . . people in lower sets weren't given.

S2:   They were treated differently to the higher attainers . . . there's that bit.

S1:   Grouping and setting limits lower ability pupils from learning more abstract branches of the subject which they may be more successful at.

S2:   And there's that bit later on – there's another bit of research – which says that low attainers are given less time to answer questions, and are given the answer before they have time to think about it – whereas with a higher level class you might say 'Well, you're not right, why don't you think about this' or have this clue whereas the low attainers are told

'That's wrong, this is the answer'.

S1:   Doesn't that define their low ability though? I mean if they didn't grasp it like in 10 to 15 minutes, how much time are you going to give them?

....

S2:   Yes, but it says that a high attaining class would be given longer to do a similar question because the teachers think they've got the mental capacity to work through it.

S3:   I would question whether it's ability per se. I would say there are other concerns the teacher will have like control.

In this taped discussion, the students did not talk about their own teaching or the practices seen in schools when referring to the issue of ability and attainment although they did use examples when discussing other issues. Perhaps some topics are too close to the bone and it is safer to engage with them at a largely intellectual and theoretical level. At the very least, it will be important for student teachers, who have no control over structures in schools, to compare their assumptions about different sets. They need to guard against low expectations, examine their own practices and try out alternatives like giving low attainers more time to answer. Moreover they need to look very carefully at the relationship between attainment and behaviour and ask:

- Is there really a strong correlation?
- If there is one, why?
- If I were in the bottom set what would I feel like?
- Does this hierarchical structure actually create problems of discipline and control?
- Is there something we can learn from other subjects?

Within-class organisation

The tension between the individual and the group which underlies the organisation of classes is carried through into the classroom, where organisation is open to several variations:

- Pupils working individually on the same topic.
- Pupils working individually on different topics.
- Pupils working cooperatively.

These broad categories cover a variety of practices and may admit of different seating arrangements. For instance, pupils may be sitting as a group around a table, talking about their work and helping each other, but the intention is that they will produce their own individual work. Alternatively, the class may be sitting in rows facing the front, and doing a short individual or paired activity which will then feed into a whole-class cooperative activity, e.g.:

Four fours – pairs combine four fours with different mathematical operations, and the class's joint efforts are agreed and tabulated. Any gaps are left as challenges.

e.g. $(4 + 4 + 4) \times 4 = 48, 4 + 4 - 4 - 4 = 0, 44 / 44 = 1, 44 / 4.4 = 10$

Small group cooperative work may involve working towards a common problem-solving goal, which may involve splitting up to work separately at times, and then coming together to discuss results.

For example, finding and classifying all the different triangles which can be made from straws of length 2 cm, 3 cm, 4 cm, 5 cm, 6 cm.

Although this form of approach has benefits in terms of attainment, self esteem, interpersonal relationships, and team work (Askew and Wiliam, 1995: 36) it is comparatively rare, perhaps because teachers remain ignorant or unconvinced of its value, or because they have not developed the skills necessary to help pupils work successfully in a cooperative way. It may be necessary to help pupils learn these skills by explicitly:

- assigning specific tasks to members of the group
- intervening to give help or to act as a mediator
- setting targets and time limits for particular phases of the activity
- expecting pupils to explain findings to each other . . . clearly.

Although mixed attainment groups can work well in this way, the type of grouping also needs care:

> . . . the optimum grouping would comprise:
>
> - 'near' mixed ability group; high-and middle attainers or middle and low-attainers
> - in mixed sex groupings, balanced numbers of boys and girls.

(Askew and Wiliam, 1995: 38)

The one-to-one situation is sometimes seem as an ideal, and numbers in a class as a barrier to learning, and while there may be occasions when both are true, there are big advantages to learning in a group which can be overlooked. Quite recently at an ATM conference I was in a session, led by Ann Watson, working on an activity from Points of Departure with three newly qualified teachers, two of whom were mature. I had had that book for ages but had never picked it up to try out some of the ideas myself. We had a lovely day working cooperatively, and at the end there were some things I wanted to work through more slowly by myself so I went off and sat under a tree in the sunshine to work. I found that I needed both to work in the group and to work individually in that order. I clearly experienced the power of the social group in bringing knowledge and experience to the learning situation, providing moral support, motivation and peer tutoring but the need to consolidate and extend individually was also important. This moving between group and individual work was a powerful combination for me in that situation.

Gender

In the past 20 years a substantial literature about 'girls and mathematics' has developed, much of it concentrating on the two perceived problems of under-achievement, and low participation after the age of 16. Explanations for this phenomenon have ether stressed inherent biological differences between the sexes, or the effects of different socialisation patterns in upbringing and in the schooling process. Biological determinism as a sole explanation is undermined, however, by the evidence of negligent sex differences in some countries compared with others, and by changes over time (Hanna, 1989). The huge social changes following the women's liberation movement and anti-discrimination law in the 1970s, greater participation in the work force, and improved educational expectations have undoubtedly contributed to this change, but the work in improving girls' experience of mathematics in schools must also be acknowledged. Making mathematics 'girl friendly' has been behind initiatives to widen contexts in texts and resources, to improve careers advice and to heighten teachers' expectations of girls (Burton, 1986; Shuard, 1981).

Against this background of social change and within education-initiatives, performance in mathematics is now very even up to the age of 16 apart from at the highest grades at GCSE, but participation post 16 is still unbalanced (Goulding, 1996). This is still seen as a greater cause for concern than boys' participation in learning modern languages in official quarters.

That mathematics acts as a critical filter for further study and future careers can not be denied, but this framing of girls as disadvantaged is problematic, since there may be very sensible reasons why they do not make an effort with mathematics and shun further study. Lesley Jones and Teresa smart (1995), leading figures in this area, put forward cogent arguments why girls are making positive choices in rejecting mathematics in favour of other fields, which may offer greater stimulation, relevance and meaningful learning experiences.

Much of the research on gender has looked at girls as an undifferentiated group, and has made generalisations which gloss over the vast differences in attainment and attitude within groups of the same sex. The great merit, though, is that looking at mathematics learning through the lens of gender can throw light upon unwritten social rules at play both inside and outside the classroom. This in turn can open our eyes to situations where it is not necessarily girls who are a disadvantaged group, but others for whom the usual learning experiences on offer are alienating. Observable and puzzling social patterns then give us the impetus to look more closely at how organisational structures and membership of social groups affect the way in which the individual can function and learn effectively. For many learners, these factors impact upon us emotionally first.

THE AFFECTIVE DOMAIN

It is a sad fact that, more than any other school subject, mathematics has the power to arouse feelings of anxiety, fear, helplessness and guilt, and that these feelings can be attributed to:

- a change of school
- promotion to higher sets
- unsympathetic teachers

- over expectation on the part of parents
- criticism
- comments about slowness
- the need to use paper and pencil and show all working neatly
- the innate characteristics of maths such as accuracy and speed.

(Cockcroft, 1982)

Since only a small correlation between attitude and attainment has been identified in some studies (Bell *et al.*, 1983), it may be argued that this is the price we have to pay for producing competent students with the requisite mathematical skills and understanding. Those of us wanting to change the culture of mathematics education, however, would counter that these experiences are neither desirable nor inevitable, but we would not want to water down the challenge of the mathematics in the process. Buxton (1981), for instance, not only gives us the conditions under which panic is induced but offers perfectly manageable strategies for overcoming these debilitating feelings:

- Conditions:
    - an inability to plan a solution to a maths problem;
    - an inability to plan a solution to a maths problem in time;
    - no expectation of being able to form a plan;
    - fear of being exposed as inadequate or foolish.
- Remedies:
    - providing students with a high level of success and a level of failure which they can tolerate;
    - when approaching a problem, students should be allowed to receive and stabilise the information before being asked to tackle the problem;
    - the process of solution to be started with full attention but slowly;
    - students encouraged to check their own solutions.

The important message here is that pupils can become more successful at learning mathematics, and this may require the explicit teaching of strategies. Learning includes change, and the belief in the possibility of change is vital. Unfortunately many pupils have learned motivational styles which close down their options and limit their opportunities, and it is the teacher's task: 'to foster a view of ability in mathematics which is changeable rather than fixed' (Askew and Wiliam, 1995: 28).

Students need to learn that they will make errors and get stuck, they will be given constructive criticism, and they will be encouraged to work accurately and precisely. Focusing on feelings does not mean making students so comfortable that they fall asleep, or making them so dependent on the teacher for unconditional praise that they cannot function without it. They need to be treated with respect and consideration, but not molly-coddled, so that they can rise to the challenges which mathematics undoubtedly offers. This requires teachers to give an appropriate blend of support and challenge, a maxim which has been used already in this book when looking at student teachers learning.

THE COGNITIVE DIMENSION

Understanding

In this discussion after an observed lesson, a student teacher remarks upon one pupil who is less acquiescent than her more biddable peers:

Tutor: I like the fact that you are going on to graphs because it can seem a very isolated thing just finding the values of functions . . . it doesn't go anywhere.

Student: I think that's the problem Kelly's having with it, She understands . . . she knows how to do it, but she doesn't understand why she should do it . . . she sort of looks at the wider picture whereas the rest all go 'this is easy, we can do this'.

This extract gives us a useful link with the previous section on the affective domain, and with the previous chapter. It is an example of a lack of functional understanding (de Villiers, 1994) – being able to do some mathematics but not knowing where it fits or what it means. Only one pupil in this class wanted to know the significance of the mathematical topic and most of the others were motivated simply by success. In fact, the simple acceptance of the curriculum by the majority of the pupils in the class is a very worrying phenomenon, although it may make for a quiet life. It may mean passive acceptance of received knowledge, which ultimately will not be helpful academically or in adult life where a critical faculty will be necessary if real choices and intelligent decisions are to be made.

Michael de Villiers argues that functional understanding should be added to the important distinction between Richard Skemp's instrumental and relational understanding (1976), in which the former refers to being able to use algorithms, rules and definitions correctly and the latter refers to the richer understanding of conceptual relationships and their logical connections.

In my experience, Skemp's article touches raw nerves with many PGCE students who read it for the first time. Some of them argue:

1. That relational understanding is desirable but may only be achieved if pupils gain instrumental understanding first.
2. There is not enough time to develop relational understanding, and instrumental understanding may be enough to get most pupils through examinations.
3. That the two go hand in hand.

Some students are still engaged with this debate later, as evidenced in this extract from an end-of-course interview:

Student: Yes, because I'm thinking about at the beginning of the course I would have been far less concerned I think about teaching them the concepts and more concerned about teaching them how to do it.

Interviewer: Well done, so you've changed.

Student: But over the course I've definitely moved towards a more developing their conceptual rather than their procedural understanding I think it's fundamental.

Interviewer: Wonderful, that is actually a very perceptive comment of yours to be perfectly honest. Although it is much more difficult to teach concepts.

Student: Yes, tell me about it (laughter). But then they understand it in the end so it's more worthwhile . . . I was taught Maths in a very tradition[al] way, we were taught methods the whole time, em and in the end I got the conceptual understanding because I was prepared to put the effort in, em so I mean some people would say that I learned in spite of the style but I'm not sure that I did, I think it's a question of attitude because if you are prepared to put the effort in you can work from the techniques and develop the understanding, but the problem is that we have a situation where, em there are two things coming into it, the first is that pupils think that Maths is where you go in and are told how to do something and you do it, the other attitude is that they are not prepared to think, so because of that we have to make them think, and that's why it is so important to develop the conceptual side, because they are not prepared to put the effort in to develop that understanding. Because if they are told they can work out the circumference of the circle by timesing the diameter by pi they are not going to worry about why, or why it works for every circle, they are just going to do it. So I think it does depend on you[r] situation and there is a place for teaching em techniques and a place for teaching concepts. The memory things are to combat specific problems for example the coordinate thing because you have, it's an arbitrary thing, they could have designed a system so that you go up and across, but it's arbitrary that it goes across and up, rather than the technique thing you know like teaching a technique for doing simultaneous equations, there are four, if you teach them one they are just going to know that one and they may not understand how a simultaneous equation works or what it means, but if you teach them four and you also give them situations where it might be used which is hard, I've heard one of a coffee shop which is quite interesting, or the puzzles, by doing more techniques and by trying to develop the concept rather than just the method, then you are developing the understanding. It's, it's the memory thing is separate from the techniques thing.

Although this student is not using Skemp's terminology it would seem he is using a similar distinction, and wrestling with the problem of how to teach for conceptual understanding. There are no easy answers.

Grey and Tall (1994) write about a 'proceptual divide', separating pupils who can use the condensed forms we find in mathematics and adapt them flexibly, from those pupils who constantly have to return to memorised procedures. For the former pupils, certain facts and relationships are available in memory and these can be used or adapted to deduce new relationships, whereas the latter group always have to start at the beginning of a known procedure and work through methodically. Common examples are:

- The over-reliance on counting – imagine trying to work out 1191 + 3, if you have to count up to 1191 before counting on the 3!
- Continued use of repeated addition instead of multiplication – even when using a calculator.

Misconceptions

In this extract, it is a problem of control for the student teacher which throws light upon cognitive difficulties which the pupils may be experiencing:

Student: But that last lesson he wasn't actually too bad he was about the only one who seemed to, willing to work. We were doing multiplying and dividing mentally by powers of ten so like 10 divided by point 2 that sort of thing.

Tutor: Yes.

Student: And they didn't understand it, and I couldn't see why they didn't understand it, some of them did, in fact most of this side of the room did but that lot I sort of said to them right we're dividing by point 2 what should we do . . . 'Divide by point 2? What's divide? Do you mean share?' and things and timesing by point 2, 10 times point 2, 'Don't know how to do that' and so I sort of spent, I'd expected this bit to be the short bit in the lesson, we'd do it at the beginning, they'd do some questions and we'd go on to a mental arithmetic test and it took the whole lesson and we only did ten questions, and I'm sure that they were just playing.

Tutor: I don't know actually because all the research shows that actually those kinds of things are very problematic.

Student: Aah.

Here, the student who was already having a hard time with this class was dismissing the genuine difficulties which some of the pupils were having as 'playing up'. She found it difficult to believe that they couldn't do what to her was straightforward arithmetic. In looking at this more closely, let us examine both the mathematics and the language used by both the pupils and the teacher. Even in an innocent question like 10 divided by 0.2 there are a host of possible pitfalls.

First of all, it looks as if this was a decontextualised question and so there were no pointers from the context which could have been helpful. For instance, if the pupils had been asked:

'How many lengths of interlining, 0.2 m long could be cut from a length of 10 m?'

the pupils may have tackled the question as a division, or they may have said 0.2, 0.4, 0.6, 0.8, 1.0 – five in a metre, so 50 in 10 m. The size of the answer may have come as no surprise given the situation. But if the question had been decontextualised, the pupils may have run up against the misconception that division makes things smaller.

Secondly, the question may have been written in several different ways:

$10 \div 0.2$, or $\dfrac{10}{0.2}$ or even $10/0.2$

and the pupils may not have known that each of these symbolic forms is equivalent. The lack of the division meaning associated with the second fractional form , in particular, is well known as a stumbling block for many pupils (Dickson *et al.*, 1984). If pupils are only used to the parts of a whole model:

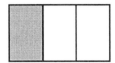

then the connection between the picture and the idea that $1/3$ also means 1 divided by 3 may not be part of the pupils' pre-knowledge. Even more problematic are fractions like $2/3$ which some pupils simply see as a visual entity

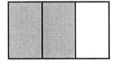

but less commonly, as a division, 2 divided by 3

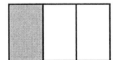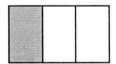

where the resultant shaded region is still $2/3$ of a unit.

Additionally of course all these fractional forms can be seen as numbers on a number line, a representation which is even less commonly held than the division form.

In returning to the extract, the language that the pupil was using – 'sharing' – betrays a partial understanding of the concept of division which will be of no use when trying to tackle 10/0.2. The idea of sharing between 0.2 of a person is clearly ludicrous.

In order to fully understand this question the idea of division as partition, i.e. how many 0.2s in 10, needs to be in place.

So although the student was disturbed by the slow rate of progress in this lesson, she has evidently not realised the complexity of the apparently simple question she was expecting the pupils to do, and she has missed the clues that the pupils were giving here in their oral language. She will not be the first inexperienced (or experienced for that matter) student to do so. Unless we as teachers really listen to pupils and sharpen our own understandings of misconceptions through reading and sharing research (e.g. Dickson *et al.*, 1984), these cognitive obstacles will remain. Pupils give us insights into their thinking with everything they say and do in the classroom, and we often fail to capitalise on them, exposing errors and dealing with them explicitly being a powerful stimulus for learning.

INTEGRATING TEACHING AND LEARNING

If learning is influenced by social, affective and cognitive dimensions then teachers clearly have to attend to all these factors in the classroom in creating learning opportunities for pupils. Barbara Jaworski (1992) offers a model of mathematics teaching, based on a study of investigative mathematics teaching, which is very helpful in linking these and other elements together:

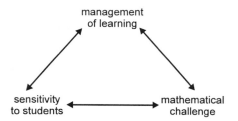

This model arose out of her study of classrooms in which a particular teaching approach was being adopted, so that she found teachers for whom:

- The management of learning involved established ways of working in the classroom, e.g. the shared expectation that pupils would ask their own questions, given a particular starting point.
- Sensitivity to students involved the ethos of the classrooms and the relationship between teachers and pupils, e.g. the tone of voice in which teachers talked to their students.
- Mathematical challenge involved offering opportunities for pupils to become engaged in mathematical thinking, e.g. stimulating pupils to extend what they had found and to look for explanations.

She links this model to constructivism, a theory which is commonly accepted, at least amongst academic mathematics educators, as an explanation of how individuals actively make sense of their experience as they learn: 'What it recognises is that learning is a constant process of meaning making, and common knowledge is a negotiated synthesis of such things.'

Note the word negotiation. It implies an interaction between pupils and teacher, where

> ... students [are] meaning makers and teachers [are] supporters of the process of meaning making by their students . . . . The teacher has a responsibility (by *law*) in some countries to deliver the curriculum. Thus the teacher would like students' construal to include meaning making relevant to that curriculum.

Jaworski gives us a few very closely observed examples of this negotiation taking place in practice, by skilful teachers working successfully at providing learning opportunities for their pupils. Other writers give us more circumspect accounts of constructivism in practice. For instance, Mike Askew, Joan Bliss and Sheila Macrae (1997) explore the constructivist metaphor of 'scaffolding', the process by which a more knowledgeable adult can help a child move from his actual developmental level to his potential developmental level, giving just enough help to enable the child to move from one to the other. Despite detailed observation and analysis of 105 lessons in primary classrooms they found very little evidence of teachers as intuitive scaffolders, and come to the conclusion that:

> Perhaps the best way to regard scaffolding is [as a way of] alerting the teacher to watch out for the extent to which pupils can succeed at tasks on their own, suppressing the desire to step in and help too soon yet being prepared to work alongside the pupil when a genuine need arises.

Other theorists may not call themselves constructivists, but in writing about teaching mathematics they have a similar view of an active learner, in the social situation of the classroom, with a purposeful teacher designing learning opportunities. Alan Bell's research (1993a) has shown that sequences of gently graded problem-solving tasks do not result in long-term learning and he goes on to propose principles, based on his own and others' research, which should underlie the design of teaching. These are:

> First one chooses a *situation* which embodies, in some *contexts*, the concepts and relations ... in which it is desired to work. Within this situation, *tasks* are proposed to the learners which bring into play the concepts and relations. It is necessary that the learner shall know when the task is correctly performed; hence some *feedback* is required. When *errors occur*, arising from *misconceptions*, it is appropriate to expose the *cognitive conflict* and to help the learner to achieve a resolution. This is one type of *intervention* ... another ... is in adjusting the *degree of challenge* . . . . The next requirement is for ways of developing a single starting point into a multiple task, bringing the learner to experience a rich variety of relations within the field ... this can be done by making *changes of element* (e.g. types of number), *structure*, and *context*. The degree of *intensity* of this complex of learning experiences is an important factor. *Reflection* and *review* are other key principles.
>
> (Bell, 1993b)

These principles involve the teacher in a rich web of activity, but the potential for pupils' involvement in the process is only clear when Bell goes on to illustrate his principles in practice. In some of the classrooms which Jaworski studied, these ways of working would be known to the pupils so that they came to expect to do certain things without the teacher having to tell them. So, for instance, they would expect to extend results – trying different types of numbers, different types of configuration, different numbers of variables. During an extended task they would expect to be called together to look back at what they had done so far, identify strategies and share results and hypotheses. At the end, a write-up would be commonplace.

To illustrate some of the principles in practice, consider the following sequence of LOGO activities (Examples 10.1 and 10.2). The pupils have done people turtle activities, and know the basic commands FD, BK, RT, LT, PU, PD. They also have some idea about angles.

It is very difficult to be prescriptive here. The design of these two simple activities and the corresponding description of how they might proceed in practice is based on my own experience of doing these activities with many different groups over many years. The point about the design, though, is that it incorporates Bell's principles but it is *flexible* and the pace and flow of the lesson is determined by the response of the learners and the decisions made in situ:

> Flexibility of task is necessary to ensure that all pupils in the class, with their varied knowledge and abilities, can find a suitable challenge within it; flexibility of intervention means that the teacher should negotiate with the pupil in the course of the task, adjusting the challenge to keep it at an appropriate level.
>
> Careful minimum interventions also encourage learners to stretch their existing knowledge as far as possible and thus to extend and enrich their conceptual network of facts, relationships and their implications, rather than to assume that each new twist of the situation requires an additional element of instruction.
>
> (Bell, 1993)

This does require the teacher to have built up a repertoire of good activities which will provide rich starting points, and to be aware themselves of the web of interconnecting concepts involved in mathematics – the very things which student teachers may only be building up slowly during their training year.

So let me finish with an example of a student teacher placed in a very typical situation on teaching practice. The scheme of work required him to teach the pupils how to solve linear algebraic equations involving brackets, and the student was very successful in demonstrating a 'method' and then giving the pupils help as they worked through graded examples from a textbook. Most pupils were managing very well (but completely flummoxed when their correct method produced $18x = 12x$). The student was happy with their success and felt that he was doing a good job in preparing them for forthcoming NC tests. What simple things could he have done to address some of the principles outlined in this chapter?

Example 10.1   Activity one – working in pairs, plan a picture on paper and use LOGO to draw it on the screen

The pupils will all draw different pictures, and may make mistakes with estimating lengths and angles and with turning the wrong way. The turtle may not do what they expected (*conflict*) but the *feedback* will be immediate, their instructions will still be visible, and this may help them to go back and correct their mistakes. If this is not obvious to the learners the teacher may help them to expose their *errors*. Since everybody will be doing slightly different things the teacher will often not know what the problem is or how it arose so the pupils will have to go back and explain what they have done, what they want to do and what has gone wrong. By communicating this to the teacher they are *reflecting* on their work, and in many cases this act of talking it through will help them to see where they have gone wrong. At this early stage corrections may involve reversing instructions and erasing lines which they have already drawn. This activity is often very *intense* with a high level of engagement from pupils wanting to produce their own pictures, and with repetition subsumed within a purposeful activity.

At some stage in the lesson, pupils may want to draw a circle. The teacher can now step in and guide them. Pupils often expect there to be a new command for drawing circles, but the teacher will need to help them see how they can draw what looks like a circle with their existing commands. She may take them away from the computer and ask them to walk through the circle using steps and turns. When they go back to the computer and try repeated steps and turns, they will soon realise how long winded this is going to be. The time is ripe for introducing the repeat command. Her two interventions are of different kinds:
1. The first encourages them to use what they already know, but to put it together in a different way.
2. Introducing some new knowledge in the form of a new command with its own particular syntax.

During the lesson, these new ideas often spread around the class. At the end, however, the teacher may leave some time for the pupils to look at each others' pictures, and encourage certain pupils to explain what they have done to the class. This may be explaining how they drew the circle, or explaining a particular difficulty which they may have had and which they have only partially sorted, e.g. getting a roof to meet up properly by trying different angles and different lengths:

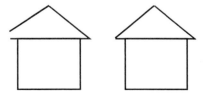

If the teacher has given enough time for this, it will be an important feature of the whole teaching unit. Not only will the pupils be practising their communication and listening skills, they will be *reflecting* on and *reviewing* their work and learning. With the help of the teacher they will be standing outside of the doing part of the activity, articulating their strategies and making connections which may not have been obvious when they were immersed in the immediacy of the task.

Example 10.2   Activity two – exploring shapes with right angles

The second activity is designed to build on the first, but to change the *structure* and *context* so that pupils deepen their understanding of some of the angle and shape properties which were present but not explicit in the first activity.

Unlike the first activity in which pupils could work towards their own goal, in this one the teacher could present a variety of challenges:

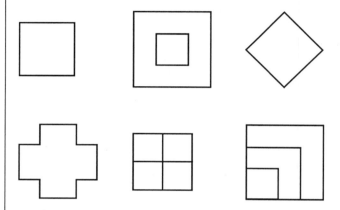

These have been specifically chosen to illustrate the logical connections which need to be made between the sides and the angles in order to draw the shapes. Further, they have been specifically designed to encourage the process of refining the sequence of commands needed to draw each. So, for instance, a square could be drawn step by step but it could also be drawn using the repeat command. If this has been introduced in the previous activity pupils may use it automatically or they could be reminded. So two sets of commands for the square may arise:

FD 100 RT 90 FD 100 RT 90 FD 100 RT 90 FD 100

REPEAT 3[FD 100 RT 90] FD 100

In the nested square shape, the orientation of the turtle after the first square has been drawn is also an opportunity for discussion. This may lead on to:

REPEAT 4[FD 100 RT 90]

By openly discussing these different forms the learners would be deepening their knowledge and making new connections.

1. He could have stressed the *meaning* of equations like:

   $2(3x + 5) = 18$

   by starting with 'Think of a number, multiply it by 3, add 5, double it and the answer is 18. What is the number?'
   (For a detailed description of this approach in practice see Hewitt, 1996.)

2. He could have asked them to draw a diagram to illustrate the equations,

   e.g. $3(x + 5) + 2(x + 1) = 21$

 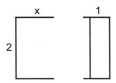

   where the total area is 21 sq. units. This is not ideal because x is an unknown quantity whereas the other measurements are known, which is why the broken line is used, but it could be used to generate discussion.

   In another lesson, this could have been extended to see if the area model will work for other equations, e.g.

   $5(x - 4) + 6(x + 7) = 11.$

3. He could have asked the pupils to substitute the answers back to see if they did satisfy the equations.

4. He could have asked the pupils to start with a numerical value, build up some equations of their own and try them out on their partners.

5. He could have started with a problem where the technique could be used. How many posts are needed in a fence with 99 panels?

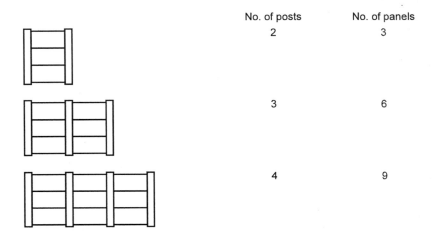

No. of posts	No. of panels
2	3
3	6
4	9

6. He could have let the pupils all become stuck on $18\,x = 12\,x$ and then used this as a focus for a whole-class discussion.

7. He could have given some worked examples, some of which were wrong, and asked the pupils to find out which were wrong and why.

$$
\begin{aligned}
\text{e.g. } 5(2 + x) - 3(x - 1) &= 6 \\
10 + 5x - 3x - 3 &= 6 \\
2\,x + 7 &= 13 \\
x &= 6.5
\end{aligned}
$$

8. He could have used some different letters and some fractional or decimal coefficients.

9. The pupils could have had a period at the end of the lesson when they classified the problems into different types, or explained their solution to the class, or identified the ones they had found difficult and why. The teacher's role could then be taken over by other pupils, who had understood these particular problems.

Several of these techniques would not require the student to stray much from the text and the examples he was using – others would rely on his knowledge of other approaches. Together, though, they present a whole set of new possibilities which move away from the transmission model which was in operation – this is how to do them, now go off and practise and I'll explain it to you when you are stuck.

CONCLUSION

We know that many learners are not successful with the traditional transmission model of teaching mathematics, and moreover that this lack of success can be very damaging in personal terms. As a short-term solution to the very real pressures of external examinations, teaching by rote is tempting, but there are other alternatives which can be used to achieve both these expedient aims and other, more general, and ultimately worthwhile aims. These recognise that knowledge is generated socially, that learners work best when they can see the point of what they are doing and feel safe enough to take risks, and that teachers can help learners to build upon and extend their present understandings over time. These are positive messages which can underpin both continued learning in mathematics and in other areas throughout the learner's life.

REFERENCES

Askew, M. and Wiliam, D. (1995) *Recent Research in Mathematics Education 5–16*. London: HMSO.
Askew, M., Bliss, J. and Macrae, S. (1997) 'Scaffolding in mathematics, science, and technology,' in MA Reader, Block IV, ME822, *Researching Mathematics Classrooms*. Buckingham: The Open University.

Backhouse, J., Haggerty, L., Pirie, S. and Stratton, J. (1992) *Improving the Learning of Mathematics*. London: Cassell.

Bell, A. (1993a) 'Some experiments in diagnostic teaching,' *Educational Studies in Mathematics,* **24**.

Bell, A. (1993b) 'Principles for the design of teaching', *Educational Studies in Mathematics,* **24**.

Bell, A.W., Costello, J. and Kuchemann, D. (1983) *A Review of Research in Mathematics Education Part A*. Berkshire: NFER-Nelson.

Burton, L. (ed.) (1986) *Girls into Maths Can Go*. London: Cassell.

Buxton, L. (1981) *Do you Panic about Maths?* London: Heinemann Educational.

Cockcroft, W.H. (1982) *Mathematics Counts. Report of the Committee of Inquiry into the Teaching of Mathematics in Schools*. London: HMSO.

de Villiers, M. (1994) 'The role and function of a hierarchical classification of quadrilaterals', *For the Learning of Mathematics,* **14**(1), 11–18.

Dickson, L., Brown, M. and Gibson, O. (1984) *Children Learning Mathematics*. London: Cassell.

Goulding, M. (1996) 'GCSE coursework in mathematics: teachers' perspectives and the performance of girls,' *Evaluation and Research in Education,* **9**(3).

Grey, E. and Tall (1994) 'Duality, ambiguity and flexibility: a 'proceptual' view of simple arithmetic', *Journal for Research in Mathematics Education,* **25**(2).

Griffin, P. (1989) 'Teaching takes place in time, learning takes place over time', *Mathematics Teaching,* **126**, 12–13.

Hanna, G. (1989) 'Mathematics achievement of girls and boys in grade eight: results from twenty countries', *Educational Studies in Mathematics,* **20**, 225–32.

Hewitt, D. (1996) 'Mathematical fluency: the nature of practice and the role of subordination', *For the Learning of Mathematics* (in press).

Jaworski, B. (1992) 'Mathematics teaching: what is it?' *For the Learning of Mathematics,* **12** (1), 8–14.

Jones, L. and Smart, T. (1995) 'Confidence and Mathematics: a gender issue?', *Gender and Education,* **7**(2), 157–66.

Lorenz, J.H. (1982) 'On some psychological aspects of mathematics achievement, assessment and classroom interaction', *Educational Studies in Mathematics,* **7**(2), 157–66.

MacIntyre, D. and Brown, S. (1978) 'The conceptualisation of attainment', *British Educational Research Journal,* **4**(2), 41–50.

National Curriculum Council (1992) *Starting Out with the National Curriculum*. York: NCC.

Ruthven, K. (1987) 'Sex stereotyping in mathematics', *Educational Studies in Mathematics,* **18**.

Shuard, H. (1981) 'Differences in mathematical performance between girls and boys', in *Mathematics counts, Report of the Committee of Inquiry into the Teaching of Mathematics in Schools*, Cockcroft, W.H. (Chair), Appendix 2. London: HMSO.

Skemp, R.R. (1976) 'Relational understanding and instrumental understanding', *Mathematics Teaching,* **77**, 20–26.

Watson, A. (1996) 'Teachers' notions of mathematical ability in their pupils', *Mathematical Education Review,* **8**, 27–35.

11: Developing as a teacher

It is time to pull together some of the strands which have been running through the previous chapters. Students on a training course have precious little time to debate philosophical issues because their behaviour is characterised by action – physically moving between institutions, preparing and handing in assignments, teaching classes, marking – but there will have been moments throughout the course when a chance remark from a pupil or a recurring pattern has registered as important. Encouraging students to be reflective and critical is part of the rhetoric of teacher education, of course (Schon, 1983), but whether important shifts in learning actually take place is a moot point. Disappointingly, there is some evidence (Haggerty, 1995: 120) that general beliefs about teaching, and the nature of mathematics which students bring to the course remain resistant to change despite substantial tutor input. This may be due to recent changes in courses and an over-emphasis upon practical experience, the difficulties which new mentors have in tackling this part of the training programme, or the fact that students are so preoccupied with surviving, keeping classes under control, and being seen to be competent that other considerations pale into insignificance.

In the course of gathering the material which has been used throughout the book, my own previous awareness of these pressures has been strongly reinforced. The pressure to be seen as a competent teacher, both by the teachers in the partnership schools and by the pupils, is, in my view, the most double edged of all. In Rosalind Scott-Hodgetts' (1996) research with pupils she found that:

> Pupils of both sexes and various levels of attainment were consistent in the view that the single most important feature of the good teacher was the ability to explain the mathematics clearly and thoroughly.

Delving deeper she found that this meant 'breaking the work into small steps, repeating explanations and giving rules (short cuts)'. These strategies were successful in promoting positive attitudes, but carry with them a one-sided view about teaching and learning. My own reservations about the personal statements made by students in Chapter 1 are echoed in this research:

> ... we need to question the degree to which they are being encouraged to think deeply about the work they are undertaking and to what extent they are being guided towards more independence in their methods of learning. Overwhelmingly, the message I got from these pupils was ... that the teachers' job was to convey their knowledge and that their own role was to absorb it.

Improving pupils' confidence and attitudes to mathematics, then, can result in practices in which the pupils are entirely dependent on the teacher to deliver a teaching sequence which is easily digestible and passively received. Similar assumptions govern the structure of many teaching materials, of course, and many student teachers have managed successfully on this diet themselves. There is a temptation to say 'if it was good enough for me it will be good enough for my pupils' and to reject any alternatives out of hand. Some of the examples which I have been able to use in this book have, however, illustrated a shift in the thinking of some of the student teachers studied.

One of the functions of the training course is to give students the opportunity to consider alternative theories, whether by observing them in action in schools or by reading about them in the academic and professional literature. Being exposed to a variety of alternatives can be destabilising, however, and without a keen critical eye students can find themselves wrestling with unhelpful polarities, e.g. either the simplistic theories of teacher as expert transmitter or teacher as the facilitator of discovery (Jaworski, 1992). In finding their own personal teaching style, they often get stuck on the distinction between open-ended and closed tasks, or between coursework activities and those which are designed to prepare pupils for written examinations, almost as if these represented positions on a continuum from good to evil. In a taped discussion of journal articles, however, one student seems to be coming to conclusions about a mixed approach:

> 'it's probably the best way to let them do it – is it not – to let the children flounder initially and then to say – well like in that article – to analyse it afterwards in class.'

which relies strongly on the teacher's interventions, but which gives pupils a chance to experience the cognitive dissonance which Leon Festinger (1957) identifies as essential for learning.

In my view, trying to achieve measurable change over the training year is unrealistic since the task of effecting significant change in students' beliefs about the nature of mathematics and its teaching is a long-term project. The most that a one-year course can offer is a taste of possibilities, which can then be followed up in further courses of study, preferably not those tied to the implementation of short-term initiatives. It is also important that students realise that 'training' which is relevant and useful to them may not be in the form of a quick fix to a problem identified, but may consist of experiences which enrich them as a person:

> Practical wisdom is a matter of experiencing what is going on accurately and sensitively, of becoming (maybe slowly, over time) the kind of person who finds these things absorbing and not merely discomfiting, and who as a consequence becomes still better able to experience them more attentively.
>
> (Smith, 1996: 207)

In this journey, there is a place for both theory and practice, the school and the university, the teacher and the academic. The search for enrichment may well start with a practical problem arising for a teacher in the classroom but be pursued elsewhere. For some teachers, this may mean using their starting point to trigger a small piece of classroom-based research, either as part of a higher degree or as part of some collaborative research with an IHE. This type of project is described by Barbara Jaworski, from the University of Oxford, and Clare Lee, one of the participating teachers, in a recent edition of *Mathematics Teaching* (1997). Barbara writes:

> . . . I have come to realise the powerful potential of 'hard' questions about the reasons motivating classroom acts. Such questions cause us to go deeply into the personal theories and beliefs which are behind our classroom activities. My own research has shown that, when such questions are tackled seriously, the result is inevitable deepening of awareness and development of practice. Such development arises, not because teachers agree to try out new ways or methods, nor because some external authority requires change, but because the teachers' thinking itself moves on.

and Clare offers confirmation:

> One way that I came to understand more about the importance of research was to do it myself. Any other teacher could do the same.

Although my dream would be for every practising mathematics teacher to be offered funding and time to pursue a course of advanced study in mathematics education, I have to be realistic. If further extended study is not an option, then joining either the Mathematics Association or the Association of Teachers of Mathematics would enable the newly qualified teacher to keep in touch with debate through their regular journals and yearly conferences. At the very least, as a change from browsing through the jobs section, new mathematics teachers should read the Extra Mathematics section of the *Times Educational Supplement* which comes out about three times a year.

Throughout a teaching career, the nourishment offered by reading and shared discussion of learning can be both personally and professionally enriching, as I have found in my own, sometimes haphazard, journey. The student readers of today may find their interest in the issues of this book reawakened when they themselves become involved in mentoring new entrants to the profession. If so, they may really deepen their understanding of learning to teach mathematics.

REFERENCES

Festinger, L. (1957) *A Theory of Cognitive Dissonance*. Illinois: Row Peterson.
Haggerty, L. (1995) *New Ideas for Teacher Education: A Mathematics Framework*. London: Cassell.
Jaworski, B. (1992) 'Mathematics teaching: what is it?', *For the Learning of Mathematics*, **12**(1), 8–14.
Jaworski, B. and Lee, C. (1997) 'Teachers can do research', *Mathematics Teaching*, **158**.

Schon, D. (1983) *The Reflective Practitioner: How Professionals Think in Action*. London: Temple-Smith.

Scott-Hodgetts, R. (1996) Monograph L. *Learning Mathematics: Pupil Perspectives*. Buckingham: Open University Press

Smith, R. (1996) 'Something for the grown ups', in *The Role of Higher Education in Initial Teacher Education*, Furlong, J and Smith, R. (eds). London: Kogan Page.

Useful addresses

The Association of Teachers of Mathematics

7 Shaftesbury Street
Derby
DE23 8YB

Telephone
(24 hour answering service)
01332 346599

Web address
http://acorn.educ.nottingham.ac.uk//SchEd/pages/atm/

The Mathematical Association

259 London Road
Leicester
LE2 3BE

Telephone
0116 270 3877

Web site
http://members.aol.com/mathsassoc/MAhomepage.html

Index